LINCOLN CHRISTIAN COLLEGE / W9-BQX-038

Called for Life
Finding Meaning
in Retirement

Called for Life
Finding Meaning
in Retirement

Paul C. Clayton

THE
ALBAN
INSTITUTE
Herndon, Virginia
www.alban.org

119802

Copyright © 2008 by the Alban Institute. All rights reserved.
This material may not be photocopied or reproduced in any way
without written permission. Go to www.alban.org/permissions.asp
or write to the address below.

The Alban Institute
2121 Cooperative Way, Suite 100
Herndon, VA 20171-5370

Unless otherwise noted, all Scripture quotations are from the
New Revised Standard Version of the Bible, copyright © 1989,
Division of Christian Education of the National Council of the
Churches of Christ in the United States of America, and are used
by permission.

Cover Design by Andrea Koran.

Library of Congress Cataloging-in-Publication Data

Clayton, Paul C.
  Called for life : finding meaning in retirement / Paul C. Clayton.
    p. cm.
  Includes bibliographical references.
  ISBN 978-1-56699-365-4
  1. Clergy—Retirement. I. Title.

BV4382.C53 2008
253'.20846—dc22
                                        2008019884

    12 11 10 09 08   VG   1 2 3 4 5

CONTENTS

Acknowledgments

I am suggesting in this book that exercising our calling requires a community. That was certainly true for me in writing the book. I am grateful to a community of people who helped me.

Beth Gaede, the Alban Institute's gifted editor, heads the list. She had suggestions not only for the structure of the writing but also for the theological content of the manuscript. Jean Caffey Lyles, the copy editor, is equally gifted. Thanks to the Alban Institute for providing such high-quality editing. These two women made the book readable.

Roger Henson and Bink Garrison shared their stories of how they were called to be a firefighter and a CEO, respectively. Their participation makes this book relevant to laity as well as clergy.

Our family talked about the meaning of a calling and retirement long before a word was written. Their perspective kept me from slipping back into outmoded assumptions. The writing of our son, John, about his grandmother's death adds depth to the book.

Jackie is the center of life for me. Her support, honest criticism, profound wisdom, and deep faith characterize her life as a wife. When all that is applied to a book, the outcome is amazing.

Thank you, Jackie. Thank you, all.

Retirement: Continuing the Call

A colleague, Kim, and I fell into conversation over a cup of coffee. Kim had just retired after decades of hard work and profound growth. Eyes, face, body conveyed the deep anguish of the soul. It had become clear in the past year that the time had come to retire. At 65, Kim's pension was adequate, and colleagues had agreed that this was the time to step aside. The previous week, a farewell banquet had been held. "So what do I do now?" was the urgent question. "I no longer have a call from God, a meaningful vocation, an identity."

The ten years of my retirement have been as fulfilling as any other decade. I have grown, found satisfaction in creative new ways of living, gained control over the amount of stress in my life, and enjoyed having some free time. My enthusiasm makes Kim's questions about the future exciting, not frightening. In retirement many ask questions, each framed by a different perspective.

"Will I ever be interested in retiring?" some baby boomers ask.

"Who am I now?" newly retired clergy ask.

"What is our responsibility?" judicatory executives and CEOs ask.

"How do I deal with retired clergy who are members of my congregation?" pastors ask.

"What can I do if I disagree with the pastor of the church where we are active?"

"What, if anything, is God calling me to do and be after retirement?"

Since I am a retired pastor, I thought about writing for ordained people who ask the questions I have asked. Almost immediately I saw that retirement is basically the same experience for clergy and laypeople. Both often find it hard to break away from a full-time job, and both wonder whether they will find a way to be fulfilled in retirement. Martin Luther's doctrine of the priesthood of all believers asserts that all baptized Christians are ministers of Jesus Christ. That doctrine of lay ministry is still hard for people in our culture to accept. For centuries it was the clergy who were understood to be called. That history inhibits the idea that laypeople are called as surely as clergy. Clergy are called to participate in the saving work of God. Scientists who invent vaccines save lives. Teachers in the classroom shape the future. Police and firefighters provide security for thousands of people. Parents who nurture their children give hope to us all. Both clergy and laity are called.

Called for Life reflects on our calling in the context of our retirement. As a retired Christian pastor, I write in the context of my faith. The term "calling" is often used in a secular context to denote a passion for helping others, but it originated with Abraham and Sarah's calling from God; it is a theological term. The religious origin of a calling justifies this tie to biblical texts. However, I don't believe that God's call is limited to Christians. Every time people thought that Jesus should not associate with Gentiles, he ignored those critics, and if we assume that God will snub people who are not like us, we are in for a surprise. God doesn't fit into our neat little boxes. If any reader is interested in retirement but not in religion, I would urge that person to read on. I respect those who don't share my faith, and I ask those who don't share my theology to respect my perspective.

From my viewpoint, our call makes life meaningful, and I believe that our calling extends into our retirement years. Douglas Schuurman, professor of religion at St. Olaf College in Northfield, Minnesota, says that when college students begin to wrestle with their calling, "they are challenged to see the totality of their lives in relation to God."[1] Although Schuurman describes students searching for a career, I think he would also say that in every stage of life the search for a call is not a placement tool but a search for God.

Does it seem as though I have confused two concepts, a general call to faith and a particular call to an individual? On the one hand, some define our calling as a general, open invitation to be a follower of Jesus. There are big, global, universal teachings that define the Christian faith. At the center of our faith are the Ten Commandments (Exod. 20:1-17) and Jesus's words at the Last Supper, "This is my commandment, that you love one another as I have loved you" (John 15:12). To be called is to embrace these teachings. On the other hand, the particular call answers the question, "How does God relate to our individual lives?" But I don't think these are the same question. It's not that I've confused the two but that I believe people of faith must combine them. The point of the faith that grows out of the biblical tradition is to bless the world with our personal lives. A calling includes commandments that spell out God's relationship to us and our personal gifts with which we make a difference in the world. The big defining commandments and the urgent, personal quest together constitute a meaningful life.

In the early years of our country, people didn't retire; they worked until they fell ill or died, says Harold Koenig, associate professor at Duke Medical Center and author of *Purpose and Power in Retirement*. Sons and daughters cared for their parents when they were sick, inheriting the farm or the store when they died. By the late 1800s, everything had changed. Value and worth were measured by productivity. Seniors were in the way.[2]

In the early 1900s about one-third of men over 65 retired on Civil War pensions. Social Security was the U.S. government's response to the Great Depression, with its high unemployment and scarcity of jobs. The idea was that getting older adults out of the workforce would help free up jobs for younger people and boost the economy.[3]

World War II changed everything again. After the war, younger adults found employment far from home, leaving their parents on their own. At the same time, pensions and entitlement programs, along with improved health care, meant that older adults lived longer and were able to care for themselves. Entrepreneurs offered well-off retired people a new understanding of retirement—leisure in front of the television or in Sun City. Such a model for retirement seemed to be a victory for everyone: business boomed, younger adults felt less guilty, and retirees were free to enjoy themselves. But Koenig describes a different outcome.

> While there were positive results for some older adults who took this path, it also led many into self-absorption and prejudice, tensions with younger people, boredom and lack of a sense that they were contributing to society and to others' lives.[4]

Even in this era, not everyone fits the description of a leisurely retirement. My wife, Jackie, and I find that our parents and grandparents, in their retirement, poured their lives into part-time or volunteer work. They were fulfilled, energized, and blessed by their outreach. How do Jackie and I reconcile our parents' ongoing service with the popular image of retirement as the "golden years?" Koenig provides one answer:

Religion is a major factor in volunteering, and volunteers are much more likely to have strong moral values about helping those who suffer. Nearly 70 percent of all volunteering among older adults is done within a religious setting, and those who attend religious services are most likely to volunteer. One-third of those who do not belong to a religious organization volunteer, compared to more than 60 percent of church members.[5]

Our parents were among that 60 percent of church members who helped others in their retirement. Koenig suggests that there is a tie between those who are faithful and those who help others even in their retirement. Baby boomers insist, and many others believe, that there is more to life than playing golf and watching TV in retirement, though they may not be motivated by a religious conviction. The exciting quality shared by the new retirees is that they understand how fulfilling a vital and engaged retirement can be. This book is built on the assumption that most people don't want to spend the final third of their lives doing nothing. What they want is a life that is worth living, an occupation that will help others, a retirement in which they can continue their calling.

The years we are retired can fill one-third of our life span. In the first third of life, we learn not just arithmetic and literature; we learn how to live, how to relate to family members, how to fit in with peers. The second third of life is productive, as we nurture our children and work at our occupations. The third stage is retirement. Our increased life expectancy means that we will be retired for approximately the same number of years that we were employed. That statistic suggests that we have to worry about having enough income to last, as well as having enough meaningful activity to make these last years satisfying.

Robert G. Kemper taught me how to prepare for retirement. A United Church of Christ (UCC) pastor, he worked for several years for the UCC Pension Boards and ran retirement workshops for clergy over age fifty. I was profoundly touched by my time with him. Not only did he explain the financial choices we would have to make upon retirement; he introduced us to what he believed to be the more important question—what are you going to do with your life when you retire? In his book *Planning for Ministerial Retirement* he explains that retirement is more than one experience; he describes three stages of retirement: "The Footloose Stage, The Settled Stage, and the Sheltered Stage."[6] In the workshops he called these the "go-go," the "slow-go," and the "no-go" stages. Retirement is more than a financial arrangement; it is a large and complex third of our lives.

There is no right or wrong way to approach this third phase of life. I will use examples from my experience and from others, lay and clergy, to explore the advantages and difficulties of retirement. Our focus will be on how our calling affects this third phase of life. I hope that after you have read this book, retirement will be an exciting prospect rather than the frightening word it was for Kim. I hope you will see retirement as an opportunity to do what you have always wanted to do and to become the kind of person you have wanted to be. I hope the word "calling" will become a meaningful term that moves us all to a deeper and more sacred life experience.

CHAPTER 1

Who Is Called, by Whom, for What?

What difference does faith make in my life? Why am I here? What would God have me do or be? The answers to all of these questions are embodied in our calling; some would use the word "ministry" or "mission" rather than "calling." Others talk about God's call to us to "serve God and neighbor." From my perspective, we are all called—clergy, laity, the faithful, and the people on the fringe of a religious life. But people make many assumptions about what a call is, and many of those assumptions do not help us respond faithfully to our callings. Here are four assumptions that need to be challenged at the outset.

Assumption 1: To be called is to be employed. Many are called to be pastors, firefighters, business executives, or plumbers. That is why Kim was so concerned: If there was no job, there would be no calling. Discerning our call in retirement is not a job-placement process. Although we are called to an occupation, our calling is larger than a job. The word "vocation" comes from the Latin *vocare,* which in Latin means "to call." In the New Testament, Jesus called his disciples to follow. He promised no employment, no occupation, no clear task; they were invited simply to be disciples, learners. Over the centuries the meaning of the word "vocation" changed. The church linked the calling of the disciples to the role of clergy, to the extent that eventually the only people who were understood to be called were ordained people. The original meaning of the word "vocation" was changed by common usage over the years so that most people came to equate "calling" with "employment." "Don't worry, Kim," is my advice. "Look for the original meaning of the phrase 'called by God.'" To be called is to follow in the way, not to have a specific profession.

Assumption 2: To be called is to have had a spiritual experience. While it is often true that a calling involves a spiritual experience, two underlying assumptions need to be addressed. First, if we are called, does that mean we have heard the voice of God Almighty? Perhaps, but it might also be that God called us as he called the Twelve: through the voice of Jesus the carpenter. Many are called by God's speaking through an aunt, a teacher, a pastor, a friend, or a parent. Second, if we are called, does that mean God is now in charge of our lives? God is God. But that doesn't mean we are puppets at the end of a string. God created the world and calls us to follow by empowering us to make choices, to envision goals, and to take responsibility for our actions.

Assumption 3: To be called is to have one single direction in life. Many people feel locked for life into one task. But the disciples were called first to be followers and learners. Then, with the death and resurrection of Christ, they were to be leaders, healers, the embodiment of Christ himself. Although some encountered the risen Christ again before their change from disciple to apostle, even then it is clear that the original call to follow was part of the subsequent call to lead. Within our calling is the requirement to be open to change.

Assumption 4: To be called is to have a God-given map of life's journey. Not only do we who are called need to be flexible; we need also to be able to grope our way through chaos with no guide. Look at the book of Acts. The apostles had no advance notice of what was to happen next. Like us, they stumbled along, praying to God that they were going the right way. "Praying to God" is the point here. Being called meant that they had to stay tuned to the Spirit's leading; they had to be tuned to prayer, as Jesus had been, day by day.

A New Definition of Calling

Three components are included in our calling: our identity (our answer to the question "Who am I?"); our gifts ("What are my abilities?"); and our occupation ("What is my unique place in this crowded and complex world?"). Using Paul's call to be an apostle, let's explore these three ingredients of our calling.

> Meanwhile Saul, still breathing threats and murder against the disciples of the Lord, went to the high priest and asked him for letters to the synagogues at Damascus, so that if he found any who belonged to the Way, men or women, he might bring them bound to Jerusalem. Now as he was going along and approaching Damascus, suddenly a light from heaven flashed around him. He fell to the ground and heard a voice saying to him, "Saul, Saul, why do you persecute me?" He asked, "Who are you, Lord?" The reply came, "I am Jesus, whom you are persecuting. But get up and enter the city, and you will be told what you are to do."
>
> Acts 9:1-6

Identity

Our *identity* is a set of characteristics that make us recogniz-able, by which we are known, that make us unique. "That's Judy walking over to meet us; I'd know her anywhere." Our identity is also a set of characteristics by which we are recognized to be a member of a group. "He is Irish; his thick brogue makes it clear." Our identity is both our uniqueness and our link to a larger group of people.

The characteristics by which we recognize the identity of Paul are startling. Before his conversion, he was energetic, dedicated—we might say driven—in his resolve to capture all who followed Jesus. Later, in his newfound commitment to the Christian church, some would say he was a fanatic. Both before and after his experience on the Damascus road, I imagine, people could recognize him by his stride, his confidence, and his charisma. Paul was also connected to two very different traditions—Jewish and Greek—and he was a Roman citizen. His multicultural heritage was demonstrated by his being known by two names—Saul and Paul (Acts 13:9). Saul was the first king of Israel in the eleventh century BCE, and the name Paul came from the Latin *Paulus,* a Roman surname that must have been common in the days when Rome ruled Palestine. Even though the apostle had devoted his early years to the Jewish side of his heritage, he was also Greek. A Jew and a Greek, living in Roman-controlled Palestine—that multicultural identity gave Paul's mission breadth and depth.

While our own identities are probably not as dramatic as Paul's, each of us is recognized by our uniqueness and by our link to family, region, ethnicity, and nationality. Our identity—the way we answer the question "Who am I?"—is part of our calling. Our identity is a significant part of what we have to offer. Our identity is shaped by our life experience. An example is the stutter and severe learning disability I dealt with as a child. That handicap shaped my identity, and I now see how it opened opportunities for ministry. I know how important the church is for a parishioner with a disability. I am living proof that a failing grade isn't the end of the world. The whole of life, nature and nurture, is a gift from God. I don't mean that God inflicted the handicaps, but that those challenges shaped my life and my perspective.

Characteristics of our identity change as we mature. I was recognized by my stutter in primary school, by my laughter in college, and by my intensity as an adult. Amid our growing, developing, and shifting, however, we maintain a stable personality. God called Jeremiah, saying, "Before I formed you in the womb, I knew you, and before you were born I consecrated you; I appointed you a prophet to the nations" (Jer. 1:5). Our calling includes the whole of life, all that we have been, all that we are, all that we will become.

Gifts

By *gift*, I mean a talent, an endowment, an aptitude, or a natural ability. These capabilities are bestowed upon us by God, and no compensation is expected from us. Even if we ignore the gift, it is still there and often comes alive much later in our lives.

The life of Paul is a dramatic illustration of how we can develop and use these gifts. Paul is the one who envisioned a church that included both Jew and Greek. When that vision became a reality, it presented a nearly overwhelming challenge. Jewish and Greek cultures were profoundly different from one another. One example is seen in the issue of law and grace. The law is the guiding religious principle in Judaism. The Torah and interpretations of the Torah developed by rabbis over the centuries constituted the law. To live by the law of God was not only a duty but also a blessing. The law was a gift from God. Paul's new vision focused on grace. We are "justified by God's grace as a gift, through the redemption that is in Christ Jesus" (Rom. 3:24). Paul insisted that the law still stands, and that grace now reigns. He argued against those who believed they could earn God's favor by their obedience to the law, and he opposed the assumption that only law-abiding Jewish people were counted as God's people. He was both Jew and Gentile. He valued the law as God's gift to Israel, and he believed that those who were not Jewish were justified by the gift of God's grace. The Jerusalem meeting of apostles and elders arrived at a compromise between living by the Jewish law and living by the Greek cultural norms. Gentiles did not have to be circumcised before they were baptized, but they had to agree to respect the Jewish tradition by abstaining from "what has been sacrificed to idols and from blood and from what is strangled and from fornication" (Acts 15:29). With that agreement, the apostles and the elders, with the consent of the whole church, welcomed both Jew and Gentile into the church (Acts 15:22-29). But these issues didn't go away when the Jerusalem meeting adjourned. Paul struggled with the issue of law and grace for most of his life. Paul's gift was the ability to bring Jew and Greek into one church.

The second example of a challenge that Paul was uniquely gifted to address is what we believe about life after death. In those days, life after death for the Greek was understood to mean that at death the spirit left the body to be absorbed into the divine. For the Jew, body and spirit were inseparable. How could these two belief systems be joined? Watch Paul do it by moving from logic to poetry: "Flesh and blood cannot inherit the kingdom of God. . . . Listen, I will tell you a mystery! We will not all die, but we will all be changed, in a moment, in the twinkling of an eye, at the last trumpet" (1 Cor. 15:50-52).

To spread the faith beyond Judaism to the Greek world and to reconcile the conflicting assumptions of two cultures was an enormous task. When Paul had to define the faith for Jew and Gentile, his gifts became apparent—political wisdom, theological genius, pastoral instincts, and a cross-cultural perspective. All these centuries later, we stand in awe of this gifted soul.

Like Paul, we are gifted in many ways, and these gifts are part of our calling. Wolfgang Amadeus Mozart was gifted as a child. Music was his gift from birth. Yet the gift had to be developed. Mozart practiced endlessly. Our gifts need to be nourished, practiced, and honed. In my experience a gift is evident and it develops most dramatically at a time of crisis, when everything seems to depend on my ability. When conflict threatened a congregation I was serving, I developed leadership skills that affirmed both sides of a conflict while we found a way to move forward as one church. If Mozart was like most of us, an approaching concert was what forced him to perfection. In the absence of crisis, some motivating force is needed to push us to develop our God-given abilities.

The link between identity and gift is clear. Both are bestowed upon us by God's grace; both grow and develop; both are ingredients of our calling. But they are also distinct from each other. Identity is that which makes one recognizable as a unique person and as one who shares a common heritage with a larger community. Our gift is the talent, aptitude, or ability that was bestowed upon us from the beginning and in the course of life. Thanks be to God for both identity and gifts!

Occupation

Occupation has several definitions. We occupy a dwelling, a residence, a workplace. "He occupies the house on Pine Street." "To occupy" is also to seize control, to maintain the land. "Rome occupied Palestine." Still again, one can occupy an office or position. "She occupies the pulpit at First Church." All these definitions focus on place. Our calling is also about a place in the world—not in the geographical but in the theological sense of the word. God makes room for us on the ground, a place for us in history, a role for us in the community. When God called Abram, God said, "Go from your country and your kindred and your father's house to the land that I will show you. I will make of you a great nation, and I will bless you and make your name great, so that you will be a blessing" (Gen. 12:1-2). Abram was to vacate his place in Haran, and occupy the land God would show him. That "place" was a moving target. Without a map, Abram and Sarai went from Haran to Shechem, and from there to Bethel, and "Abram journeyed on by stages toward the Negeb" (Gen. 12:9).

Like Abram and Sarai we journey on by stages toward the Negeb. We catch a glimpse of what seems right for us, settle down in the relative comfort of that occupation, only to move on to another place in our journey, and another after that. Abram's call was to the whole journey. The one call included Shechem, Bethel, and the Negeb. Our occupation might include several places, churches, positions, or careers, from childhood through retirement. Our occupation might evolve from student, to employee, to parent, to volunteer. Our call might include two or more occupations at the same time. The call is not to a specific occupation but to a pilgrimage in which one venture may lead to another.

"What is the destination of this pilgrimage? When do we arrive? Where is the Negeb?" you might ask. In the days of Abram and Sarai the Negeb was a large area of Canaan, just another stop along the way. The point of God's call is not that we will arrive at some blessed location at the end of the journey. The blessing comes along the way, as part of the pilgrimage. The Negeb is simply another huge district. When we arrive there, we find it is just another place from which we continue the journey. The trek is like climbing Mount Washington in New Hampshire. For an hour we hike toward the summit that we think we can see directly above us, only to find, when we arrive there, that it is one of many outcroppings along the trail. When we finally do reach the summit, we see a whole line of mountains, the Presidential Range, marking the fault line, waiting for us to occupy them as well. It is along the way that we are rewarded with vistas of glory.

Abraham and Sarah were the first people to understand that there was one God; they were the first to be called by this God, called to be a blessing to all the families of the earth. Abraham and Sarah represent a new beginning for all of us in the traditions of Judaism, Christianity, and Islam. We are indeed blessed by those first pioneers. In a sense our call is part of their call, to go "to the land that I will show you" (Gen. 12:1).

An Authentic Calling

Identity, giftedness, and occupation are ingredients of a calling. Having defined a call, how can we be sure that it is a call from God and not something we created on our own? How do we measure the authenticity of a call?

In my college days I worked summers at Morgan Construction Company. The company's purpose was to build steel mills. My job was to sweep the floor and run errands. During those summers I learned that I didn't want to do that job all my life and that studying for finals was preferable to sweeping the factory floor. But I also learned that these men who labored in the factory were fascinating. Those who operated lathes ground huge blocks of metal into precise, polished parts for the final mill. Those who assembled pieces to make a machine were imaginative and knew exactly what the final product would look like.

Were any of these factory workers called? The answer to that question is "They loved their neighbors." The community there extended even to folk like me. If I came in a couple of minutes late, everybody banged on sheets of metal with huge hammers to announce my tardiness. That was embarrassing, yet rewarding—they saw me as one of them. People reached out to one another; some had an amazing ability to be neighbors, mentors, pastors to others. I came to understand also that these factory workers had a life after they left the factory floor. One of my friends there was the janitor at the Roman Catholic parish where he had grown up. He saw himself as a part of the ministry to that congregation. Another sang with the town chorale and felt he was a part of an effort to make something beautiful. From where I stand, it seems that they were called as surely as any pastor I know.

But how do we know when a call is really of God? Is there an objective criterion that helps us see the difference between a great job opportunity and a genuine call from God? I think the Genesis account of the rainbow covenant helps answer those questions.

The Noah story begins with these words: "Now the earth was corrupt in God's sight, and the earth was filled with violence. . . . And God said to Noah, 'I have determined to make an end of all flesh, for the earth is filled with violence'" (Gen. 6:11-13). Noah was called to build an ark to save a remnant of every species, so that all would not be lost forever. When the waters receded, God established a covenant with Noah and his descendents: God would never again create a flood to destroy the earth. God said, "When the bow is in the clouds, I will see it and remember the everlasting covenant between God and every living creature of all flesh that is on the earth" (Gen. 9:16). Walter Brueggemann, an Old Testament authority, observed the importance of this ancient tale. "On the basis of God's 'never again,' the rainbow covenant was established. . . . The promise of God is that [God] will never again be provoked to [destroy the earth], no matter how provocative . . . creation becomes."[1] That "never again" promise stands behind the call of Abraham and the creation of Israel and Islam. That "never again" promise stands behind the birth of Jesus and the church. The purpose of God is never again to destroy but again and again to call people and institutions to share in that saving work, so that God will not have to break that "never again" rainbow covenant.

The call of God is always consistent with God's saving purpose. Is this an authentic call? If this pilgrimage means that we are to share in the saving work of God begun with Noah, that we are to share in the saving work of Christ described in the New Testament, then the call is authentic indeed. The distinctive mark of a calling is not the nature of the work but the purpose of the worker.

My Favorite Biblical Sentence

The most remarkable sentence in the Bible is found in the Genesis story of Abraham and Sarah. God called Abram to go from Haran "to a land that I will show you." I've been to Haran. It was a terrifying move God was asking of Abram and Sarai. The ruins indicate that Haran was a large and sophisticated city on the edge of a desert. God called them to leave their home and go to "a place that I will show you." That call went against their identity as a wealthy urban couple. That call to a new occupation in an unknown place was outrageous. That call to live a gypsy life in the desert was unthinkable. The most remarkable sentence in the Bible begins this way, "So Abram went . . ." (Gen. 12:4). As a result, we are all blessed and called to be a blessing.

For Reflection

- What do you think is the distinction between a job and a calling?
- How would you describe your identity, your gifts, and your occupation?
- If you thought your calling was to the U.S. Senate, how would you know it was a genuine calling and not a hunger for power?
- During which periods of your life so far have you felt closest to your calling?

CHAPTER 2

Finding
Our Real
Selves

A calling is not the result of an employment interview or a business plan. It is a matter of discovering ourselves, our real selves. In this search for self-identity, we are seduced by promoters who urge us to move to Sun City and enjoy a do-nothing retirement, or to buy into consumerism and enjoy shopping, or to build our portfolio large enough that we'll never have to worry. God calls us in a different direction. We are encouraged, instead of getting more and more for ourselves, to give something of ourselves to others.

Our calling is our identity, our giftedness, and our occupation; all combine to make our calling. In this chapter we are struggling with the discernment of that call, the discovery of ourselves, what it is we have to give to others. That is not an easy task. Since it is God's call, the discovery is a theological task. As we move from school to occupation to retirement, our calling shifts as well. In this chapter three other people and I share our self-discovery, our search for a call. Roger Henson has been fire chief in towns in California, Massachusetts, and Rhode Island. Jacklyn Blake Clayton is my wife, an educator, author, and homemaker. Bink Garrison is senior vice president at Vertex Pharmaceuticals, Inc., in Cambridge, Massachusetts.

I offer first our four stories, and then some thoughts on how they reflect the definition of a calling.

My Story

My story goes this way. I grew up with a bad stutter that isolated me from my peers. Looking back, it is clear to me that I also had a learning disability; today it would be diagnosed as dyslexia. One day when I was 14, the pastor, John Martin, came to our house to talk with my mother, who chaired the Christian education committee. When they had finished their conversation, Mother called me: "Paul, Reverend Martin is leaving; come down to say good-bye." When I arrived at the door, the pastor, speaking to Mother over my head, said, "You know, Mildred, I think Paul would be a great minister." And he left. The two of us laughed out loud. Who ever heard of a minister who couldn't speak or read?

I was still a nonreader as a high-school junior, so my parents pulled together the money to send me to Kimball Union Academy in Meriden, New Hampshire. The son of my father's best friend taught there, and the school focused on underachievers. I loved Mother and Dad and my life in West Boylston, Massachusetts, but I hated school and my stutter so much that I was glad to try something new. I moved to a dormitory at KUA to repeat my junior year. I loved the place. Peers and faculty accepted me, stutter and all. Mrs. Brewster, wife of the headmaster, met with me for an hour every day. She taught me how to read. Her approach was not to fix the learning problem but to help me find a way around it. By the end of the first year the stutter had eased dramatically, and in the second year my grades were in the top 20 percent of the class.

I applied to three colleges and was accepted at my favorite, Middlebury College. I went there for all the wrong reasons: The ski slope was practically on campus, the college was coeducational, and a small Vermont town seemed like heaven. All through college, I compared every other occupation to the ministry. A lawyer makes more money than a pastor, so I majored in political science. When reading legal briefs didn't work for me, I decided that businesses paid better than congregations, so I added business administration as a minor.

My favorite professor at Middlebury College was D. K. Smith. He once confided to the class that his priority was to be in touch with college students. His calling was not the subject matter but the students he worked with. He lived out that calling by being open to individual students and by opening most classes with an informal exchange. He'd ask what we thought about the football game or describe how he had spent his weekend. Then he would turn to economic theory or accounting. Over the course of the year, we heard the details of the construction of his new home. The following September he invited a few of us to his house for a meeting. I was shocked by what I saw there. There were beds for everyone, and the kitchen was furnished—but the rest of the house was empty! A graduate of Harvard University, and the best professor I had ever known, Dr. Smith didn't have enough money to furnish his new home. From that moment on, money was no longer the controlling criterion in my search for a career. Liberated from the question of "who makes more than whom," I was free to listen to my heart. In that moment I knew I was called to pastoral ministry. I called John Martin to arrange a time to meet. He was the first person I told of my decision to be a pastor. Remembering the conversation about ministry, years before in our front hall, he was delighted, as you can imagine, and my family was equally excited.

I loved Andover Newton Theological School. The students were dedicated but wildly different, a mix of brilliant, athletic, serious, and comic. Three students in my class were women preparing to be Christian educators; we who were preparing for ordination were all men, right out of college. The faculty members were great teachers who were eager to know each of us personally.

In 1959 I began the search for my first parish. One placement officer spoke for all when he said, "Come back and see me when you are engaged to be married, and I will be able to help you." But one area minister ignored the fact that I was single and said he had just the church for me. A month after that conversation, I began my ministry in Orange, Massachusetts. It was a wretched old town with a wonderful small church—a congregation that taught me almost all I needed to know to be a pastor. I was ordained on November 15, 1959.

Roger's Story

Listen to how Roger Henson describes his call to be a firefighter.

After three years of college, I took a break to get married. The plan was for me to work while my wife, Dianna, finished her final year of college, and then she would work while I finished my architecture degree. Plans changed, however, when our daughter was born and we realized that Dianna would need an additional year to graduate. Meanwhile, I continued working at the Goodyear Tire and Rubber Company. Production was running at full capacity, requiring all shifts to work thirteen days on before getting one Sunday off. It was dirty, hard, physical work.

One beautiful June morning after work that second summer, I drove to the beach to swim, lie in the sun, and catch some sleep. There I saw an old friend from high school who said he had become a firefighter. He said, "You can't believe this job. We work a twenty-four-hour shift and are busy with various duties during the day. But after dinner, if there are no emergencies, we play basketball, pool, or cards; watch TV; and go to bed after nine o'clock. I do that every other day for three days and then get three days off." All I could think was "Where do I sign up?"—to which he replied, "The City of Santa Fe Springs is giving a firefighter's entrance test. Why not take it?" I turned in an application, and a few weeks later, he and I rode our motorcycles to Santa Fe Springs to find that 311 other guys were there to take the written portion of the exam—for two openings! My friend had led me to believe that I'd be a shoo-in and that the process would be easy. It was anything but. Amazingly, after a comprehensive and competitive five-part ordeal, I was one of the two immediately hired. Eventually, a total of four were hired from that list, but I was the only one who had not been a firefighter previously. For someone like me to get this position was against all odds. God was at work, though I didn't realize it yet.

I had joined the fire service for all the wrong reasons. I planned to be there only until my wife could graduate and get a job, so that I could resume my education. That rookie year was hazing season in the firehouse, and everyone had license. I was fair game and the butt of many jokes—some very funny, a few not so funny. Fortunately, the shift battalion chief was a stoic old guy who apparently liked the way I endured so much hazing; he would intervene occasionally with a few well-chosen words. In retrospect, that hazing prepared me for the emotional control that I would need to think clearly during and after some of the most gut-wrenching scenes that firefighters must encounter.

Attending the fire academy that year, I was surprised to find the subject matter interesting and challenging. I studied hard and graduated at the top of my class, earning the "Honor Cadet" award. At the end of one year I saw that there was more to the fire service than I had ever imagined.

The second year, I really became a firefighter and began to fit in with the program. I also began enjoying the camaraderie of the firefighters and felt gratified to help others. Although I didn't consciously give up on architecture, I did decide to continue with the fire service a little longer, even though Dianna had graduated and could now go to work. I was having fun. The calling I heard was gradual; although it was a distant sound at first, it was becoming louder. I took more classes and received a degree in fire science.

I was on the fire engine most of the time, and I loved it! Promoted to engineer (the driver/pump operator) in year four, I was then selected to train as one of the first paramedics for our department and in the nation. It was all very new. The public was not yet aware of the fire department's new emergency medical service, and much of our job those first years was public education. Almost every evening we gave talks and demonstrations to any club or civic or church group that would listen. Since we were the first city fire department in southeast Los Angeles County to provide paramedic service, we also responded to other cities for mutual aid and were kept very busy. Days off were now spent sleeping. We were finally trained and equipped to make a real difference. We did—and it felt good! I could now hear God's call as a roar.

When I was promoted to captain, I was rotated off of the paramedic squad so that I could be in charge of an engine company. Negotiating labor contracts, coordinating emergency preparedness for the city, and administering departmental training prepared the way for my promotion to battalion chief.

After twenty years, I was eligible for retirement and thought I was ready for it. I was forty-two. So I went to work for a friend in consumer electronics—but felt no call. I really missed the fire service. What did I miss? I missed being in a place where I could make the difference of death, handicap, or full recovery. Arriving at the scene of incredible chaos and leading others to resolve the emergency were also challenging. And I especially missed the camaraderie and teamwork. I therefore decided to rejoin the fire service and to apply for positions as fire chief.

God was still calling me—this time to Wellfleet, Massachusetts. The Wellfleet Board of Fire Engineers wanted me to "professionalize" the mostly volunteer department, and after four years we had achieved more than I had originally expected. My final call was to Barrington, Rhode Island, where I spent seven and a half years as fire chief.

Thirty-five years after learning about the fire service that day at the beach, and after many great rewards, some sorrow, a few injuries, and a lot of wonderful memories, I retired, this time for good and with the feeling that my fire-service calling was complete.

Jackie's Story

This is how my wife, Jackie, tells her story.

I was born and brought up on the mission field in Turkey, where my parents were educational missionaries of the American Board of Commissioners for Foreign Mission (ABCFM), a predecessor of the United Church of Christ. My parents' philosophy of becoming integrated into the community meant that my first friends were Turkish, my first language was Turkish, and my elementary schooling was in a Turkish public school. Since my parents and other teachers from the United States always spoke to me in English, I grew up bilingual and bicultural.

During my junior year in college at Oberlin, Ohio, I became keenly aware of two instincts that were stronger than ever: I wanted to work overseas, and I wanted to get into some profession other than teaching. Four out of our five family members were educators, and I thought that was enough! In my junior year, I attended a "Career Day" seminar looking into work with the U.S. Foreign Service. I discovered that I did not want that either. The agency's prohibition on interaction with local people grated against my sensibilities and sharpened my focus. I gave up my opposition to teaching and applied to the foreign-mission arm of the United Church of Christ. I was the third generation in our family to do so. I went to teach English as a foreign language in a school for girls in a suburb of Istanbul. My commissioning service as a missionary was also the 150th anniversary celebration

of the ABCFM. At that service, my calling to return to Turkey
and the story of the church's years of courageous mission came
together. I went to Üsküdar as a concrete expression of my faith
that all people the world over were God's children and that I
wished to help them through my teaching of English.

The second phase of my adult life started with marriage
and the subsequent arrival of children. I remember saying to my
elder brother that I had never before felt as sure of a decision
as I was of this one to marry Paul. Perhaps that was a way God
was telling me that I was still following my calling, despite the
move from Istanbul to Orange, Massachusetts. I don't know that
I could actually say I felt called by God to be a full-time mother,
but again I felt strongly that I was taking the right step. In those
early days of the feminist movement, staying home with children
was seen as neglecting your true calling, your gifts. Furthermore,
my mother had felt called to be a "professional woman." As the
principal of a school for Turkish girls in Izmir, Turkey, she urged
graduating seniors not to get married right out of high school
(a common progression in those days), but to go on to higher
education or a career. Maternal expectation and cultural pressure
weighed heavily on me. Despite this opposition, I felt guided to
stay home with our children. I have been deeply grateful over the
years that I had a husband who supported my decision, that we
were able to finance that choice, and that I followed that inner
voice again for such a rewarding experience.

My volunteer work during those years was with children
who were deaf and who therefore spoke a different language from
the rest of society. After our own children were in late-elemen-
tary and middle school, the exhilaration of teaching English as
a foreign language in Üsküdar propelled me to look into that
field. In those years, English as a Second Language (ESL) or
English Language Learners programs were not yet very common.
However, a small program had started in our town, and it needed
a teacher for kindergarten and elementary school classes. After

about twelve years of working with students from all over the world, I began to feel that some of these students' problems in the mainstream classroom were similar to my own experiences when I came to the United States for high school and college without any linguistic issues. This time, I remember feeling strongly that God was calling me to explore these nonlinguistic forces—a call that would entail going for a doctorate at age fifty. As I mulled over this prospect, I investigated a doctoral program at Boston University School of Education. Although the chair of the department cautioned me against this path because she saw no practical outcome for me, I persisted. I felt I had to do it. As a final blessing to the venture, a publishing house accepted my dissertation, with appropriate changes, for publication. I ended up teaching in that same department, working in the TESOL (Teaching English to Speakers of Other Languages) program with students from all over the world for many years.

Another phase of my calling has occurred in retirement. Paul had been urging me to write a book on one of my courses. I had resisted: I was not a writer, as were the other members of the family. However, once again I felt God calling me to continue my integration of culture and education. Like Moses, I offered one excuse after another. And yet, once again I felt compelled to follow through. I believe my call has been the same one expressed in a variety of ways.

Bink's Story

Bink Garrison is senior vice president at Vertex Pharmaceuticals. Bink's story can best be told by looking at the interview I had with him in his office.

Paul: How did you get where you are?
Bink: I had no intention of moving to this place. Consulting was the perfect place for me. I opened a business of my own and

called it "Bink.Inc." My personal mission was to help CEOs and colleagues get what they wanted in this world. I really feel joy when I help other people achieve their agenda. One of the clients of "Bink.Inc" was Vertex Pharmaceuticals. I helped the company build a vision, a mission, and a set of core values. My calling came when the CEO said, "I wish you could work in Vertex." "Absolutely not," I said. "Consulting is my vision." After I said "No" six times, he said, "I know you will be a terrific consultant, but you can't do what I need to do from the outside. I need you here every day so that you are in the fabric of the place. I know you love what you're doing, but if I'm successful I'm going to save about a million lives. And what are you doing?" That was the call that I had to answer, and I am so glad that I did. My title is "catalyst." Is that a calling? I think so.

Paul: You were a CEO, then worked in advertising, then served as a consultant; and now you're a vice president. How do all these occupations relate to one another?

Bink: The link in each case is creatively solving problems. In advertising, it was bringing new ads into being, but that morphed quickly into motivating people to do things in a better way. Our clients did great things in the world—T.J. Maxx, Fidelity, Raytheon. More and more my role in the advertising business was to be an adviser to the executive officers. At "Bink. Inc" that became the main function.

Paul: When you were in your thirties you had a serious illness. How did that relate to this call?

Bink: Well, I think the gift of melanoma back when I was thirty-one was this: "OK, are you doing what you love? Because you might not be around tomorrow, don't waste a single day." That lesson, "Selfishly insist on joy," has been a gift that has stayed with me.

Paul: What is this catalyst role?

Bink: I am one of the top six executives of the company. Anyone can come in here to ask for help or to get something off his or her chest. I'm the resident shrink. They might say, "My team isn't working well. Will you take us off-site and help us glimpse a vision?" or "How can we improve our relation with the FDA?"

Paul: Sounds like a chaplain's role!

Bink: On the pastoral side, along with the CEO, I'm the keeper of the vision and the core values of the company. The vision of the company is to innovate, redefine health, and transform lives. The values are these: innovation is our life blood, we need to pursue excellence fearlessly, and "We win" (not me, but we). So if I'm a pastor, those are my sermons.

Paul: So in your fifty-eighth year, you've thought about it. You love this job. What are you going to do when you retire?

Bink: Well, yeah. Why retire? So . . .

Paul: So basically you're not going to retire?

Bink: Well, yeah, there'll come a time, I suppose, when there'll be some sort of scaling back, but the core thing that I like to do is helping people, and I'll continue to do that. If they want me, I'll do it here. If not, I have a lot of opportunities in Boston. I hope to do that as long as I have the energy to do it.

Paul: If you were to continue working, would it be full time?

Bink: When I was with "Bink.Inc." I was full time, and I played a lot of golf. The management—that was me—the management was very accepting there. The management here is a little more disciplined. Golf is a wonderful diversion, a wonderful release from everyday activities, but golf every day is a hellish nightmare, especially if you play like me.

Four Stories and the Definition of a Calling

Let us see how these four stories coincide with the threefold definition of a calling.

Identity, who we are, is the starting place for all of us. Identity is what makes us recognizable; identity also links us to family, peers, or ethnic groups. Three factors shaped my identity. First, my stutter left a mark on me. To this day I am shaped by the reality of my childhood. Second, the church was a powerful influence. My mother spent a lot of time with her friends in the church kitchen, and as a child I was often there, drawing a picture or doing my homework. As a teenager, I found that the church was the only place where I felt accepted. John Martin's suggestion that I would be a good minister didn't come out of the blue; he saw me at church regularly. Third, D. K. Smith, my professsor, was an important influence on me. His new home furnished with the bare necessities ended the power that money had over me. I am sure I was influenced by my father's sad experience in the Depression; I saw how he was always worried about money. D. K. Smith's freedom to put his purpose ahead of his income liberated me.

When Roger Henson retired at 42, he missed the firefighter's life because he could make the difference between someone's life or death, recovery or permanent handicap. He also missed the camaraderie and teamwork. The power to make a difference and his commitment to peers shaped Roger's identity.

Jackie's life as a bilingual and bicultural person is central to her identity. She says, "I would have lived a different life if I had not grown up in Turkey." Her decision to be a stay-at-home mom went against her mother's preference and the social prejudice against women who gave up a career for their children. Children and biculturalism have been her identifying marks from college through retirement.

"Melanoma's lesson" stands at the beginning of Bink Garrison's call: "Selfishly insist on joy." As he grew, that lesson shifted to "I really feel joy when I help other people." The melanoma and what he learned from it shaped his personal values. Joy in helping others became his calling. I think he stutters and stammers when asked about retirement because his work is his life, his identity.

Gifts, the second piece of the definition of our calling, develop along with identity. By gift, I mean the talent, aptitude, and ability that we were born with or that we developed along the way. Roger learned the whole spectrum of the trade, from paramedic skills to emergency preparedness to management techniques. Although he says his life as a firefighter is complete, I think he will be searching for a way to continue some part of that occupation in retirement. Jackie's gift is her understanding and ability to teach children and cross-cultural teachers. Her gift as a mother is amazing to those of us who know her. As a junior in high school, I didn't know how to read but, with the help of many, I ended up with a doctorate. Bink's imaginative ability to put himself into the life of the other person is a gift. He can see everything at once—the dream, the burden, the powerful moment of opportunity.

The third ingredient in our calling is *occupation*—the place, the ground God provides for us to live and work; the transition from one occupation to another occurs again and again in life. Bink "morphed" from one role to another. As president of the advertising company, he found himself talking with clients—not about the promotion of their product but about the management issues they faced. It was just a matter of time before he left advertising, became a consultant, and then moved to Vertex. Roger moved from architectural student to firefighter to fire chief. Jackie's place in the world shifted her work from teacher to wife, mother, professor, and author. As an ESL teacher for children in kindergarten through fifth grade, she also helped classroom teachers adjust to cultural diversity in their classrooms. Many of their questions were not linguistic but cultural. That's why she moved from language teaching to a professorship, and then to the role of author in the discipline of cross-cultural living. A calling is not a job; it is a lifelong pilgrimage. Our development as we move from one occupation to another means that when we retire, we can continue our calling in a different way.

A Calling and the Awareness of God

These four stories raise the question of the relationship between calling and faith. Jackie and I both grew up in the church. Religion came first, and our calling followed. Roger's calling began with a calculation of days off; Bink's began with a resolve: "Selfishly insist on joy." They recognized the call of God in retrospect. Can there be a call if there is no awareness of the God who does the calling? That is a very complicated and controversial question. "Calling" is a biblical word. In the Old Testament God called prophets; in the New Testament Jesus called the disciples. We need to be as clear as possible about the relationship between faith and calling. How pious must you be to be called?

First, we need to ask who this God is. I believe questions, doubts, and uncertainty are part of the faith. Some say they don't believe in a God who sits on a cloud in heaven, or inflicts people with cancer, or decides it is time for us to die, or knows when we are born what is going to happen to us for the rest of our lives. I don't believe in that God either. Our understanding of God needs to change as we grow up, and that happens only when we doubt the God of our childhood. Religion without doubt can be fanaticism. When we are no longer sure about God, that doesn't necessarily mean we are agnostics; it may mean that we are growing in our faith.

Others say they believe in God but not in organized religion. The question behind that conviction is "What happened to bring you to that place?" Imagine a woman who was confirmed in 1970 at the age of fifteen. A year later her parents no longer attended church, and neither did she. Now she is forty and wonders if there might be a God, but she isn't going to go to church to find out. Another example is the man who stopped going to church when he left home. His parents' religion wasn't his, and he never found another. Still again, here is a man who served as a lay leader in the church for all of his adult life and then dropped out of the church suddenly and permanently. Are these people aware of God? We need to talk at length with them before we can know.

Can any of the people I have described above be "called"? If someone grew up in a family that didn't go to church or synagogue, that never imagined anything spiritual, can that person be called? My answer is "yes," "no," and "It's not for me to say."

The answer is yes, because often our call comes before our commitment to the faith. First Isaiah was called; then he became a prophet. First the disciples were called, and then they learned who Jesus was. First the saints were called, and then they transformed the church and the world. The calling is often the way people come into the faith. The answer is also yes because people who really don't like synagogues and churches can be called. We are here today because brave people were tired of the small-mindedness of religious leaders and set the world on fire by reforming the church.

Does God call people who are not baptized Christians? My answer is yes. Abraham, Sarah, Moses, Isaiah, and Jeremiah all were called. Ishmael, the son of Abraham and Hagar, links Muslims to Abraham. Judaism, Christianity, and Islam inherit Abraham's blessing and call to be a blessing to "all the families of the earth" (Gen. 12:3).

Does God's call reach other religions? I still say yes. Jesus healed the child of the Syrophoenician woman (Mark 7:24-30). He engaged the woman at the well in a meaningful dialogue (John 4:7-30). We are asked to follow the example of the Samaritan who helped the victim on the road to Jericho (Luke 10:30-37). "Jews and proselytes, Cretans and Arabs" (Acts 2:10-11) were all there at the first Pentecost when the Holy Spirit came upon them. It would not be out of character for God to call someone without requiring a change of religious affiliation.

The call extends beyond our assumed boundaries. We might not use religious terms to describe this call. I think most of us have sensed the meaning-filled way in which we are called to live our lives. The decisive question is how we respond to that call. Have we said yes to God's affirmation and challenge? From our innermost self, have we committed ourselves to the call to love God and neighbor? That is the question each of us must answer. Our response is the measure of the authenticity of our calling.

The Power of Simplicity

All of these complex questions about our calling are difficult. It's important to struggle with them in the context of the story. Here is a story of Jesus calling the disciples.

> As [Jesus] walked by the Sea of Galilee, he saw two brothers, Simon, who is called Peter, and Andrew his brother, casting a net into the sea—for they were fishermen. And he said to them, "Follow me, and I will make you fish for people." Immediately they left their nets and followed him. As he went from there, he saw two other brothers, James son of Zebedee and his brother John, in the boat with their father Zebedee, mending their nets, and he called them. Immediately they left the boat and their father, and followed him.
>
> Matthew 4:18-22

This enormous transformation of the lives of these first disciples cannot be exaggerated. They left everything and followed Jesus. That choice not only changed their lives; it changed everything that has happened ever since. Without the disciples there would have been no memory of Jesus. But this remarkable calling did not come with a dramatic vision of God, high and lifted up. It was a simple, ordinary conversation; Jesus said, "Follow me," and "Immediately they left their nets and followed."

So the simple conversation may transform us all: a pastor's offhand comment to my mother at the front door; a description of the firefighter's leisure time; the Foreign Service representative's disdain for friendship with nationals. A simple incident can change everything.

We are often called the way the disciples were called—with a single simple, casual comment. It is amazing when we have the courage to leave our nets immediately and follow.

For Reflection

- What did you learn about yourself in each of these four stories?
- Does the progression from one occupation to another within one calling ring true in your experience?
- What do you think is the relationship between calling and an awareness of God?
- Write your story of how you have been called.

CHAPTER 3

Community

Our calling and retirement are strengthened by a faithful community. John Martin spoke for the church community when he suggested that I would be a good pastor. Roger learned the discipline of his career from the community in which he worked. The 150th anniversary celebration of the American Board, where Jackie was commissioned as a missionary, confirmed her calling. Bink's success is based on his knowledge of the Boston business community. We discern our calling with the help of our communities. Throughout our lives, we are supported by family and friends. Since I have retired, finding and sustaining a community has been a priority. Our individualistic culture affirms the lifestyle of the Lone Ranger. The truth is that we need one another from birth to death, from adolescence to retirement. "Hermit" and "calling" are not compatible terms; calling and community go together.

What is a community? Of course, it is the friends we see regularly at church or at work or in the neighborhood. What we need to do to be helpful to them is often clear to us, and they understand what we need from them. But community also includes people we seldom see. Jackie's parents were career missionaries in Turkey. They created a global community through their correspondence. Since sometimes they were asked to work in different mission stations, they wrote letters to each other—as well as to missionaries around the world, and to people they met

at summer camps or churches where they were guest preachers. When they were in an automobile accident, when she was
diagnosed with cancer, when he grieved after her death, this
community poured love into phone calls, letters, or visits. Jackie
and I seldom see some of our very best friends—people we met
in college, in seminary, in a former congregation, or on a trip to
Turkey. We keep in touch; sometimes we e-mail them before the
New Year or telephone in midsummer or write a long, rambling
letter with no agenda at all. When we do see each other, it is
startling how we pick up from where we left off months or years
ago. Along with people we see every day or week, these friends
who live far away are also our community.

A community is able to meet our several needs. Sometimes
we need support from people who are on our side. We need
someone who is our cheerleader when we are down, someone
who can finish the sentence we began, someone who never gives
advice unless asked for it. We also need the challenge of people
who see life from a different perspective. We need a community
that includes people who were brought up in a family very different from ours, someone who usually holds an opinion opposite
to ours. We need someone who is willing to speak the hard
truths—for example, "I know how much you love your home,
but it's time to think about an assisted-living apartment." We
need someone who is able to forgive us when we have wronged
her or him and someone who is able to confront us when we are
too certain that we are completely right. We need a community
when we are depressed because we didn't get the job, or ecstatic
with the birth of a grandchild, or lonely with no one who will
listen, or overwhelmed by the sunset and longing for someone
with whom we can share the wonder of it.

The Shut-in Caucus

As a pastor, whenever I got worn down, I spent
an afternoon visiting elderly "shut-ins," who because of frailty

or illness never got out of their homes. Some clergy hate those visits because they hear over and over again the same stories about grandchildren, the same complaints about church, the same brokenhearted memories of lost loved ones. I loved visiting because of the community! With just a little nudge, the conversation turned to current events, theological insights, and outrageous humor. By suppertime, I was renewed; in bringing a new perspective to these shut-ins, I found that they had also brought a new perspective to me.

In one congregation, eight elderly women became unforgettable to me. I soon learned that they talked to one another on the telephone every day. If in any given week I visited one of them without seeing them all, I was in trouble. I called them "The Shut-in Caucus," because in each visit it became clear what issues they had agreed to "help the pastor with." They ministered to me and the church by explaining their viewpoint. Their confinement at home meant that they couldn't voice their opinions at a church meeting or in the church parking lot where decisions were made. I valued their perspective and therefore welcomed their lobbying, which meant they prepared for every visit from me with an agenda.

These shut-ins were blessed with both friendship and hope. My ministry to them included an informal research project. Each month, year after year, I knocked at each door asking myself, "I wonder if she has lost hope yet?" With few exceptions, the answer was clear: hope prevailed. No matter how glum the diagnosis, how painful the night, how limited the future, they always found something or someone worth living for. There was no question how they managed to be so brave. They made frequent telephone calls and encouraged one another through that network. In time, this disciplined telephone conversation included the agenda not only for my visit but also for my personal well-being. All these women were called to minister to one another and to me. The "Shut-in Caucus" was a community for us all.

I saw a connection between the "Shut-in Caucus" and my confirmation class. In teaching confirmation classes, I often explained that the fourth-century conversion of Emperor Constantine changed what it meant to be in the church. Before Constantine, it was dangerous to be a Christian; people were sent to jail for being followers of Jesus. After Constantine, belonging to a church was good for business; it was beneficial to have the same religion as the emperor. The confirmation class always wanted to live in the post-Constantine era. Naturally at age fourteen, a time when fitting in with peers was a priority, the young people in confirmation class wanted to be part of a popular church. I tried to convince them that hard times deepen the Christian community, that when sad or tragic things happen, the church is at its best.

Put the story of the "Shut-in Caucus" alongside the confirmation-class lesson. The eight women were pre-Constantine Christians. They were at risk, acquainted with suffering; they grieved the loss of friends again and again. In a way, the pain they all experienced tied them together into this telephone community. The ninth graders in confirmation class also talked on the phone every day but seemed to lack a deep sense of community. Was that because they didn't share the suffering of the early church? Such an assumption would be dramatically mistaken, in my view. Listen to these teenagers. A classmate committed suicide last year; Joan's mother died last week; the alcoholism of Frank's father is terrifying and without end. When a pastor, counselor, teacher, or friend listens, these confirmands embrace community as eagerly as the pre-Constantine followers of Jesus.

Mentoring and Community

These days a church I once served no longer asks its pastor to teach the confirmation class. A team of mentors representing the whole congregation leads the class. Students and adults meet one-on-one and also as a group. The confirmands get to know the church firsthand instead of from the pastor's description of it. I think that's a great idea. It means that students know people who have experienced the sad and tragic events of life; confirmands see how the church community helps and how it is helped by hardships.

The word "mentor" comes from a figure in Greek mythology—Mentor, a friend of Ulysses. Mentor stood in for Ulysses when Ulysses was away at war. In the myth the goddess Athena worked through Mentor to care for Telemachus, the son of Ulysses.[1] In our time we understand a mentor as a friendly advisor, a trusted counselor, a wise "uncle." There has been at least one mentor in every community I have known. It might be the pastor of a church, but more likely it is the youth advisor or an insightful coach who is respected by everyone in town.

Two months after I began as a new pastor, fresh out of seminary, my neighbor, whom I had been helping with a listening ear and an occasional gift from the discretionary fund, committed suicide. A month later the treasurer of the church was arrested for stealing funds from the church. Leslie Dunstan, one of my professors at Andover Newton, was the mentor who walked me through the tragedies. He didn't teach me how to deal with my doubts or help the victims. He showed me how to build a community that could support those who grieved the loss of a young son and a community that could help the former treasurer back to a meaningful life.

When I was a director of the national mission board of the United Church of Christ, Telfer Mook, the mission secretary for Southern Asia, took directors on a five-week trip to India and Sri Lanka. Jackie joined me on the bus, train, plane, and oxcart that carried us from Delhi to Colombo. We visited a couple who were both doctors devoted to the problems of poor families in isolated villages. They met with the leaders to ask what the village needed. Most often it was clean water. The doctors helped the villagers dig a well and, in so doing, tackled the cause of much illness and death—an unsafe water supply. Instead of waiting for villagers to come to the hospital, the two doctors went to the villages. Instead of curing patients one by one, they addressed the root cause of the illness.

I sat on this or that mission board for the rest of my career—and I always remembered the lessons learned from Telfer Mook. The two doctors believed that healing was accomplished by the community as well as by individual medical interventions, and thus that their task was not only to help the victims one by one but also to enable the community to be the healing agent. Healing happens when a mentor helps the community see its calling. The doctors who helped that village helped me in my congregation. When I came home from that journey to India and Sri Lanka, I saw, for the first time, how hard I had tried to keep the programs of my predecessor alive and well instead of asking if a different strategy would more adequately meet new needs. Leslie Dunstan and Telfer Mook showed me how to be the mentor to my congregation, so that the whole church community could minister to those in need.

Community and Individualism

Individualism is a force deep in our cultural and national lives. The pioneering spirit is alive and well. The history of our country makes that spirit real and concrete. Mayflower passengers, organizers of wagon trains, immigrants from Europe, Gold Rush daredevils—all were ready to venture forth into a new life. People brought up on farms or in city slums could make it to the corner office. The myths highlight the power of the individual.

In my career as a pastor, I tried to remind members of the suburban congregations I served that we might not be as self-sufficient as we liked to think. After the Second World War, returning soldiers were helped to move into the middle class by the GI Bill, which financed college educations and home mortgages. I don't think I persuaded anyone. The pioneer myth remains alive and well; even when the statistics are clear that the rich get richer and the poor fall deeper into misery, the myth lives on.

The secular religion of our day confirms the myth of individualism. In our culture, many people want spirituality without organized religion and without community. They pick pieces of many religions—a spoonful of Buddhism, a pinch of Hinduism, a full quart of Judaism, and in some recipes, a little Christianity. It's as if each person wants to own his or her calling without reference to any organized faith community. Is it possible for an individual to have spirituality that doesn't include a community?

Christianity is a communal rather than an individualized faith. The incarnation is at the core of our faith: "God was in Christ, reconciling the world" (2 Cor. 5:19). Paul understood the church to be the body of Christ (1 Cor. 12:27). The church, the faith community, is the incarnation of the Spirit. That church includes rich and poor, longtime members and newcomers, people of every race, ethnicity, and lifestyle. It isn't that we choose our community. The community, the body of Christ, chooses us. The faith community is the embodiment of Christ to us.

Community and calling go together. Having said that, I must hasten to acknowledge that while we need community, we also often resist it. I decided that the ordained ministry was right for me. I confirmed that choice with my pastor, and only then did I tell my parents. It was important for me to be sure I was making the right decision before sharing it with anyone else. Along with two of her colleagues, Jackie and I planned a trip through the Near East in 1961 in the belief that traveling together is a valid test of a relationship. I told friends and family about the trip but not the agenda. Why did I make these major decisions without consulting or even informing the community that loved me? In part it was because I grew up in an individualistic culture where we are thought to be solely responsible for our own decisions. In retrospect, I think it was also insecurity that motivated my isolation. All of my friends were indifferent or hostile toward religion. I needed to be sure of myself before sharing my intent to seek ordination, because I assumed that this choice would end my friendship with them. Throughout my young-adult life, relationships with women had been heartbreaking, and I saw no reason why my love for Jackie would have a different outcome. I needed to be sure it would work before telling anyone. My own decision to be a pastor or to marry Jackie needed to be settled before I included the community.

While I wanted to be absolutely sure before sharing my thoughts and feelings with others, the individual in me who didn't trust the community was itself created by community. The community shaped my identity: John Martin spoke for the church when he made his outrageous suggestion that I would be a good minister; my parents found the money to send me to Kimball Union Academy; Leslie Dunstan and Telfer Mook taught me how to lead. The insecurity that led me to keep the community at arm's length and the dramatic gifts that came from the wider community competed within me.

That struggle between acting out of pure individualism and embracing community simmers within most of us. We each choose our path, and at each fork we decide again which way to go, sometimes with and sometimes against the recommendation of friends and family. It took courage for Jackie to go against her mother's preference, for Roger to give up architecture, for Bink to sell the advertising company and start a consulting firm with no guarantee of success. These courageous endeavors were possible because Jackie, Roger, and Bink had all been blessed by a community, sometimes in the person of a mentor, and with that blessing they were able to follow their chosen paths.

For me as an insecure young person, the influence of the community was a saving grace, but not all communities are redemptive. Some spouses are abusive; some parents teach materialism and greed; some communities are violent gangs. We each need to choose a support system that is compatible with the core values of our calling, even if it means abandoning the community that is destructive. While that is rationally obvious, it can be emotionally difficult to turn away from the advice of the old gang, a well-intentioned parent, or a counselor from the past. The inner struggle between the old ties and the new endures from adolescence to retirement. Hard as moving to a new community can be, it is an experience we all share. When we leave home as young adults, when we graduate and launch out on our own, when a beloved spouse dies and we are alone again—these hard adjustments require new communities as well as the old ones. Clearly we need each other; we need a community from the beginning to the end of life.

Community and Authority

An authority is not only the one who is in charge but also the one who is an accepted source, one whose word is believed to be true. Throughout our lives, we search for the truth. In the political debate, which side is right? As we look for our calling, which path is best for us? Every day, at the edge of our consciousness looms the question, "How does this action fit my personal set of values?" Our search for the truth, the right way, the ethical standard is a search for authority.

One of the strongest women in my congregation committed suicide. Smart, mature, well-connected, Ann was among the first people to whom I would go for advice. She had moved to Rhode Island to be near her son and his family. During her annual check-up, the doctor found what turned out to be a malignant tumor. With that news, she pulled down the garage door, started the car engine, and died of carbon monoxide poisoning. All who knew her agreed that what she did was a terrible mistake. There was every reason to believe she would have lived a good and helpful life for many months, if not years.

Some people think we need rules to direct us to true and wise decisions. A feeding tube kept Terri Schiavo alive. The family of this young woman in a persistent vegetative state was not of a single mind. Her husband thought that because she was brain-dead, her feeding tube should be removed. Her parents thought removing the tube would be murder. The issue went to the floor of the U.S. Congress. The search for a ruling from the government meant that the family disagreement became a national issue.

Both of these tragedies cried out for a strong community. Ann never consulted her communities. She never shared her anxiety with her family, with the medical experts, with the pastor or friends in the church. A five-minute conversation with someone in any one of her loving communities could well have saved her life. The wishes of Terri Schiavo's husband and parents were set aside so that someone in Washington, D.C., who didn't know her could write a rule to save her life. When we were born, a community of people was needed to get us past the first months of life, and we have been dependent on loving communities ever since.

"How do we know the truth?" For me, that is a theological question: "How do we know God's will?" We can never know what God is thinking. Whenever someone claims to have an inside line to God, disaster is the result. To claim to know everything God is thinking is idolatry. But three windows allow some rays of light to shine in the night, so that we catch a glimpse of the truth. One is our experience. What we have learned from parents, from peers, from defeats and victories—that is experience. When we prayed, when we were at worship, when we felt deep inside that this was the right choice—those experiences were a hint of God's truth. A second window to God is the church community. We have faith because the church gave us the New Testament, it gives us a worldview, and it ministers to us every day of our lives. The close friends whom we trust, the study group that meets regularly, the insight of a grown child—all are elements of a community through which we see an edge of God's truth. The third window is the Scripture. We glimpse the truth in biblical stories told for generations, translated into every language, and applicable to every circumstance. The Bible keeps the church community from claiming that it has an inside line to God, and the Reformation insisted that the church live by the biblical truths. Scripture also reveals God's truth to each of us. None of us will ever be absolutely sure what God wants us to do at 10:00 a.m. on Thursday, but all of us can endure the darkest night with the light of the Spirit that shines through these three windows. The problem for Ann and for Terri Schiavo was that, for one reason or another, the community wasn't there when darkness fell.

My theology tells me that our choice of communities is a matter of life and death. It wasn't enough that Ann was wise and mature. It wasn't enough that the president of the United States tried to help Terri Schiavo. Everyone needs a community, a family, a doctor, a mentor, a close friend. We need strong communities so that when the night falls we will have a window open to God's blessing.

The Pentecost Community

The disciples were broken by the crucifixion, and some of them went back to their fishing boats as if Jesus had never called them. It was the presence of the risen Christ in the upper room and by the seashore that changed them from followers to leaders. The Pentecost experience provided the followers of Jesus a community after the crucifixion. Luke describes that community:

All who believed were together and had all things in common;
they would sell their possessions and goods and distribute the
proceeds to all, as any had need. Day by day, as they spent much
time together in the temple, they broke bread at home and ate
their food with glad and generous hearts.

Acts 2:44-46

Not many of us will sell all we have and pool our resources.
But we long for a community that, day by day, is dedicated to
the needs of all. Pentecost is the story not only of the birth of
the church but also of the gift of the Holy Spirit; the two go
together. The Pentecost experience is the affirmation of Abraham, who was called to be blessed and to be a blessing to all;
the call of the disciples who followed Jesus with courage; and
the call of each of us to be people of the Spirit. Pentecost gives
us a mission, a passion, and an affirmation of a meaningful life
in a world that is driven by fear. The Spirit of Pentecost that
sent the apostles into the whole world to transform and to save,
that enabled disciples to become apostles, also brings newness
of life to us.

For Reflection

- Describe the community that has been or is still a blessing for you.
- Who were the mentors who helped shape your life
  story?
- What stories characterize your struggle with individualism
  and community?
- How will retirement change your relationship to community?

CHAPTER 4

Ebb Tide:
The Transition
to Retirement

Jackie and I live on the edge of a saltwater marsh here on Cape Cod. The changes in seasons, weather, and tides make the marsh different every day. The tide is predictable. It is higher when the moon is closer to us and higher still when, twice a year, the moon and planets line up and pull the sea closer to them. Sometimes, in a northeast storm, the wind blows the sea into the marsh for days, so that there is no low tide. Ebb tide occurs when the water flows from high tide to low. Visitors prefer high tide when the water view is obvious. But at low tide birds crowd in to fish when they can reach the eels at the bottom of the marsh. The full green, orange, and red of the marsh show off as the tide wanes. We prefer the lower tide when the marsh is more engaging, yet in all honesty, no one can dislike the tide at any moment of the day.

The tides require us to change the way we live. At the tide's highest, we can paddle our canoe right across the marsh to the sea; at mid-tide, we must follow the meandering channels. It's like a maze with some channels ending in cul-de-sacs, others winding their way toward the sea. At low tide there is not enough water to float the canoe. As months and years go by, the channels change, the sandbars move, and we paddle a different route to the sea. Keep that image in mind as we explore the changes life requires in retirement, life's ebb tide, when the flow of life moves out toward the sea. That is depressing for some, but living on the marsh teaches us that the low tide is as exciting as the high.

The hardest part of any transition is surprise. When an unexpected challenge jumps in front of us, the transition is harder. If we can anticipate it, however, we can more easily cope with it. The image of the changing tide can help us prepare for retirement. It reminds us that retirement is part of the ebb and flow of life, not a sudden tsunami. If we sit down and think about retirement, attend some workshops, read some books, and talk with family and friends about the life change, we can use the old to learn the new. We can use what we learned before retirement to adjust to the new lifestyle.

The Line between Professional and Private Life

The most important lesson I learned in parish ministry, a lesson I am still drawing on in retirement, came as I began my second pastorate. I was thirty-three years old. This is the way I described it in *Letters to Lee*, a book for pastors in their first parish that I wrote in 1999.

There was a very strong woman who was in charge of the youth ministry in the church. I tried in every way to share that ministry with her, with no success. . . . "These are my kids, not yours," she said. As I watched her encourage the young people to be dependent on her, I began to feel this turf war was sick. I talked with the committee responsible for the youth ministry. That committee joined me in talking with her, asking other advisors to join her, and in every way possible tried to overcome the barrier between her and me. Nothing worked. At the end of the year, the committee members and I were unanimous. We told her she would not be advisor in the fall. She declared war on me. "If I go, I will make sure you go, too."

That was the worst summer of my life. We were expecting our second child in September. I was sure this woman could deliver on her promise to end my ministry in that church. I was papering and painting the nursery in the parsonage one August afternoon. The man who had volunteered to join this woman in advising the youth was sitting on a stool listening to me vent my fury and worry. I heard myself say to him: "My life is the ministry. If she ends my ministry, she ends my life." I saw the folly of the words the moment they were spoken. If I left the ministry I would still be husband and father; I would still be me. I could make a living some other way. In that moment I understood the difference between public and private life; the distinction between my job and my identity; the separation of my work and myself. In that moment I was free—free to risk my ministry for what I felt was right.

The committee and I stuck to our guns. She left her position as youth advisor. Her war against me fizzled; she never did have any power over me, except in my own mind. I tell this story with deep sadness. She left the church that fall, and died suddenly the next spring. I wonder how the story would have ended if I had known in the beginning what I learned in the end. If I had recognized the boundary between my ministry and my life at the beginning, would she have behaved differently? I think both of us had the same problem. We both believed our life depended on our ministry in that church. If I had been free of that idolatry, I might have been able to liberate her. But we'll never know.[1]

That experience taught me to see the difference between my professional and my private life. Deep inside, like Kim, I had linked my identity with my ministry. When I said, "If she ends my ministry, she ends my life," I suddenly understood how wrong that reaction was. In equating my occupation with my identity, I was off balance. That realization when I was thirty-three made leaving the parish ministry for retirement at age sixty-four much easier. Kim had not made that distinction, and that made retirement more difficult.

What Motivates Us Before and After Retirement

Another awareness about ourselves that we might have developed earlier in life, one that can be useful in retirement, has to do with our motivation. Psychologist David McClelland says he believes that "a person's motivation and effectiveness can be increased through an environment, which provides them with their ideal mix of each of the three needs"—the needs for affiliation, power, and achievement. These needs can be described quite simply:

- The need for affiliation. The need for friendly interactions, popularity, and a deep sense of community make people with this need good team players.
- The need for power. Some people feel a need for personal power over others—not a desirable quality. Others desire institutional power, seeking to direct the efforts of the team—a positive contribution to the community.
- The need for achievement. Some need to excel and succeed; they enjoy working on their own and don't need praise. Their achievement is all the reward they need.[2]

McClelland's theory is recognized and has provided the foundation for other important work, such as Daniel Goleman's exploration of emotional intelligence. McClelland created a Thematic Apperception Test (TAT) that measures the inclination of applicants and employees, so that their leadership can be understood and enhanced.

McClelland used this research to improve leadership. I think it can also enhance retirement. If we understand our need for affiliation, power, or achievement, we can shape our retirement to meet that need. The volunteer assignments, the groups we join, the hobbies we develop will be different for each motivating inclination. In planning for the retirement that is ahead of us, we need to recognize what has motivated us in the years preceding retirement.

Leadership Style

In retirement, we are still essentially the same persons we were twenty or even fifty years ago, but the tide has turned. We each decide which channel to paddle down—the same old one or the new trickle that was formed over the winter. I know a retired executive who found a position on a board of directors that will give her institutional power. Another plays golf with retired executives and maintains an affiliation with peers. Another gives her life as a volunteer at a charity and enjoys the nonprofit's achievements. Those who run the business and those who sweep the floor face the same choice upon retirement. The motivation that kept them moving before retirement still moves them downstream. Power, affiliation, and achievement that worked before will work after retirement. But when we retire, we can no longer paddle the straight line across the marsh; we must choose a channel and maneuver our way more carefully in the ebb tide. This transition from open water to meandering creek is like what it means to retire. It's the same life; but it is life after the changed tide.

I believe the change of tide is a blessing. Before we retired, most of us paddled against the tide. The decision of the human resources department, or the requirements of the search committee, or the needs of the institution challenged us. We drove hard against the competition and cut every corner possible. Retirement is the ebb-tide moment when we can stop striving for a place in the market and begin choosing our own channel. When we retire, the title doesn't shape us any longer. "Dr.," "the Rev.," "Prof.," plumber, CPA, or sales representative—titles or labels don't matter anymore. We can find in ourselves the answers to these two questions: What from the old life do we want to preserve? And what in this new circumstance would we like to embrace?

In the ebb tide I realized that I was still called, still blessed, still forgiven, still free to be the person that, deep in my heart, I believe I am called to be. Retirement is choosing a creek and paddling downstream, with the tide. Instead of pulling against the flow, we can steer our way with the tide that is so strong that we must follow it, or so gentle that we can enjoy the life of the marsh on our way.

Resources for the Journey

A clear understanding of our personal motivations will help us choose the channels we travel in retirement. Other aspects of our experience will also serve as valuable resources to us, however. Indeed, we may find we want to explore and strengthen these resources as we move forward.

Self-Respect

I served suburban churches for thirty-two of my thirty-seven years in parish ministry. These congregations were made up mostly of middle-class, educated, progressive people. There were always people in the minority, but the large majority supported Martin Luther King, Jr., and women's right to be ordained; and after I retired, most of those parishioners favored same-gender marriage. They were thirty-two wonderful years, because I fit right in with the congregations I served.

In retirement, we belong to a small congregation that is not suburban. While no one has opposed teaching evolution in public schools, people of every persuasion imaginable are members of this congregation. No consensus prevails on how to interpret the Bible or how to vote in a national election. At an annual meeting, the church council moved that we adopt this statement of welcome:

> As a congregation which covenants to walk together in Christian love,
> believes that all persons are created equal before God,
> and affirms the inclusive love of Jesus Christ,
> we welcome to our work and worship all people
> regardless of race, gender, age, ethnicity, sexual orientation,
> ability or economic circumstance.[3]

The motion passed unanimously. How could that have happened? The truth was that four or five families, knowing that the majority would favor the motion, stayed home. Some people said, "Wasn't that nice of them to let it pass unanimously?" I think it was sad. Different opinions are more important than unanimity. The amazing and mistaken idea was that some people assumed they should stay home rather than voice their minority viewpoint.

In the protests against the Vietnam War, teenagers and elderly people walked hand in hand at protest marches. The explanation was that the young and the old were not constrained by the need to earn a living. I think young and old were also filled with enough self-respect to stand in protest against the majority viewpoint. Those were the years when students were standing up for all sorts of change in our society, and seniors in their retirement were free to do the same. As the tide turns in our time, I sense the same independent spirit, the same self-respect among our students and seniors. May that be so!

A Sense of Rhythms

We retirees joke about the fact that we don't know what day it is. It's true because of what Bob Kemper calls "rhythms of life." The change of seasons, the six o'clock news, the monthly haircut—those are the rhythms, the markers of time. For the clergy, it is the liturgical year; for the teacher, it is holidays; for the accountant, it is often April 15; for the retailer, it is Christmas-shopping season; for the farmer it is planting season and harvest time. We enjoy not having those rhythms during vacation. Who cares if it's Thursday or Friday on Cape Cod? No one cares while on vacation, but we who live here year-round need those markers to keep us from boredom and depression. Since no staff meetings or final exams impose these markers on us in our retirement, we must invent our own.

The experienced retiree keeps the calendar full of all kinds of "dates." To quote Bob Kemper, "In time you, too, will utter the retiree's cliche, 'I don't know when I had time to work.' Translation: I did not know there were other satisfying rhythms in life besides those of work."[4]

Transparency

Once while I was serving my first church, I was washing the windows of the garage. I heard my neighbor calling to her husband, "Bill, what's Paul doing?" Bill answered, "He's washing the windows of his garage." She answered, "What's he doing that for? We never look through those windows."[5]

That conversation didn't trouble us. I grew up in a small town, and Jackie grew up in a mission station; we were used to people peering into our private lives. We believe that clean windows make for a powerful witness. If our purpose is to share the Christian life with our neighbors, then we need to live open and transparent lives. There are things that need to be kept private—intimacies within the family and pastoral confidences. But keeping windows clean so the community can look through goes with the territory.

Our transparent witness will inevitably reveal inconsistencies between what we say and the way we live. That is not a catastrophe; it's an opportunity for us to deal with our imperfections and to help others do the same. We need to develop an inner confidence that our weakness as well as our strength is part of the witness. That's not an easy requirement. We who have lived through many such embarrassing revelations of hypocrisy should be able to demonstrate the power of grace. In the upper room Peter said he would never fall away from Jesus; but in the courtyard outside the high priest's house after Jesus had been arrested, Peter said he didn't know who Jesus was. Yet Peter was the rock, the leader of the early church, the saint. In his weakness was his strength, and that strength was the steadfast love of God.

Marriage

I realize that some readers are single. And I know that the active role of the "clergy spouse" is outdated. But I have noticed that marriages may either find renewal or fall apart when one partner retires. The state of one's marriage is an important ingredient in the transition to retirement.

A generation ago, Bob Kemper described "the minister's wife" as a job title. The seminaries were graduating larger numbers of women than previously, and more were being called into pastoral ministry when he wrote *Planning for Ministerial Retirement* in 1988, but at that date, not many women were retiring from the ministry. When I went to a workshop he led in 1982, wives were invited to attend with their husbands who were considering retirement. In that context, Kemper said, "The primary compensation for the minister's wife was not money but status."[6] When her husband retired, she was not only out of work; she was out of status. Today the pastor's spouse, who may be male, often has a full-time job outside the church and that spouse, whether male or female, likely has no clear-cut function in the church. But the status issue continues for the pastor and, in some cases, for the spouse as well. The pastor's retirement can carry a loss of status.

Instead of grieving the loss of standing in the church community, a couple can use retirement as an opportunity to deepen
their love for one another. The rhythms, the work patterns, the
limitations and liberties are all different in the moment we retire. In the moment of change we can be open, transparent, and
vulnerable to one another. The ebb tide invites us to discover
a new way through the marsh grass, and a new trust in each
other. If we miss this time for reflection and renewed vows, we
will find life to be simply shallow. Retirement is a time when,
with some thought and sensitivity, we can embrace a new life
together.

Claiming a Piece of the Horizon

Whatever personal resources we draw on, we
need to move forward with a sense of personal power and the
confidence that we can make choices about our daily activities
and our future. Harvey Cox is a professor of Christian ethics at
Harvard Divinity School. Back in 1967, he wrote a wonderful
book, *On Not Leaving It to the Snake*. It is relevant to our calling
and our retirement.

> I believe a careful examination of biblical sources will indicate
> that [our] most debilitating proclivity is not [our] pride. It is
> not [our] attempt to be more than a man [or a woman]. Rather
> it is [our] sloth, [our] unwillingness to be everything [we were]
> intended to be. . . . Sloth is admittedly an ugly word. In English
> it has come to mean indolence or laziness. It is the name given
> to an unattractive animal who likes to hang inertly from tree
> branches.[7]

Harvey Cox is speaking of the creation story in Genesis (Gen.
3:1-7). We usually think of pride as the villain in the garden.
Adam and Eve ate the forbidden fruit, hoping to become as
wise as God; and that ambition, that hubris was the sin. Cox is

looking at a different interpretation of the text: "Before [Eve] reached for the fruit she had already surrendered her position of power and responsibility over one of the animals, the serpent, and let it tell her what to do."[8]

Adam and Eve were the first human beings in all creation. They had talked with God, their Creator, and they understood what God wanted. The problem wasn't that Eve disobeyed God's rule about the tree. The problem was that she let the snake decide whether she should eat the forbidden fruit. The danger in retirement is not only our pride in what we have done, but also our inclination to let chance decide how we will live the rest of our lives. By refusing to take responsibility for our future, we miss our calling. Sloth is letting the snake decide what we will do with the rest of our lives.

The urgent point of retirement is here in the creation story. Retirement is the opportunity we are given to claim a piece of the horizon. It is possible for us to choose our place in the future. If we follow the calling into this new environment, it can be like a garden. Choose a spot on the horizon instead of hanging out in the tree branches.

The ebb tide, the transition, is a way to look at retirement. If we are to stay afloat, we must choose the channel that will bring us not to a cul-de-sac but to the open sea. Since we might well live into our nineties, this transition could define the next third of our life. This is not an opportunity to be wasted.

For Reflection

- What about life before retirement will enable or hinder the new life that is before you?
- As the tide of life changes, what do you dread or eagerly anticipate?
- What is the snake in your life that wants to decide your future for you?
- What do you want to do in the rest of your life?

CHAPTER 5

Don't Just
Stand There,
Do Something

"Doing something" is a requirement for a healthy retirement. Sitting in front of the television is bad for our health. According to an article in *US News and World Report:*

Complete retirement leads to an 11 percent decline in mental health, an 8 percent increase in illness, and a 23 percent increase in difficulty performing daily activities over a six-year period, according to Dhaval Dave of the National Bureau of Economic Research and Bentley College.[1]

An article in *Business Week* looks at the benefits of work:

There is growing evidence that people who work during the years typically spent in retirement live longer than those who do not. . . . That doesn't mean you have to remain in a full-time job or career track to reap the health and longevity. . . . Just 100 hours per year of work is all that is required. Nor is it necessary to receive a paycheck: Several studies have shown that volunteerism has the same benefit as paid work does.[2]

Gene Cohen, professor at George Washington University Medical Center, co-founded the Creativity Discovery Corps at the university in 1997. He found that creative activity benefits the elderly. A more vigorous immune system, enhanced social engagement, and diminished visits to physicians all result from activity that requires learning, imagination, and creativity.[3]

The admonition "Don't just stand there—do something" encapsulates the principle that activity is good not only for our health, but also for our souls. The question is, what do we want to do in retirement? In what way do we hope our calling will continue in our retirement?

One Person's Retirement Choices

In 1996 I retired at the age of sixty-four. I had a clear vision of my first five years of retirement. I wanted to continue my ministry in the church but not as pastor of a congregation. I dedicated the first five years to passing the discipline of parish ministry on to the next generation. To that end, I wrote *Letters to Lee: Mentoring the New Minister.* I also became special assistant to the president at Andover Newton Theological School. That volunteer position was sweet indeed. I spent two or three days a week doing whatever needed to be done in exchange for an apartment on campus. In 1999 I became the coordinator of a "visioning process" for the school. Because the process was funded by the Lilly Endowment, I received a salary. The job was high-stress; I found more conflict in the seminary than in any congregation I had served, but it was a great experience that by 2002 had resulted in real change in the seminary. Those six years were what I call a "bridge" from parish ministry to retirement. We continued to have an apartment a few miles from my last parish and with easy access to Boston, but we had moved our primary residence and our church affiliation to Cape Cod.

When the seminary "visioning process" was complete and the president retired, I needed to find a new expression of my calling. The Massachusetts Conference of the UCC had called a talented young woman as conference minister and president. I suggested a couple of ways I might be helpful in conference projects. She took me up on my offer. I was also president of the Trustees of Jaffna College Funds, a mission agency that supports the work of the church in Jaffna, Sri Lanka. Those two commitments filled my life with challenge and satisfaction.

After three years the conference minister resigned to return to the parish ministry; at the same time my term on the Jaffna board ended. I was out of work again. Three projects challenged me the following year: Jackie and I worked on a history of our family that might be useful for in-laws and the next generation; our pastor and I created and taught "Bible 101" at our church; and I became a hospice volunteer. All of that was fulfilling and still is, but I was restless for something else. I submitted a proposal for this book, which became a focus for the next year. At the same time, a conference budget crisis forced the directors to reduce and reorganize the staff dramatically; instead of five associate conference ministers, there were only four. When I volunteered to help, the conference asked me to represent the conference in visits to pastors and churches so that the associate conference minister in my area would have time to get acquainted with the 30 churches newly assigned to him.

The biggest surprise and lesson about retirement for me was that I had to take the initiative. No one ever came to me to say, "Now that you are retired, would you be interested in doing this?" I was the one who invented the position, applied for it, and pressed hard against initial hesitations. I think people are nervous about volunteers. There is no way to tell ahead of time if the retired person will work out. Busy people are afraid a volunteer will be a burden rather than a help. When no one comes to ask us to do something, our first instinct is to assume that no one wants or needs us. That's not true. When you are rejected, press on—that is my advice. But if the final word is still, "Don't call me, I'll call you," learn to accept it and look elsewhere.

Keep on Keeping On

I have continued using the skills of ordained ministry, but outside the parish ministry. In this section, let me describe several other ways people remain engaged in the calling they had before retirement, and the benefits and challenges each alternative offers.

Full-time Work

Bink's choice to "work until he drops" is more and more popular: just keep on working until illness or death ends your career. His interest and passion remain high. As life expectancy increases, as more and more people feel that their work is their calling, as people feel lost without the routine of the old job, as Social Security and pension programs become less reliable, and as employers have more difficulty replacing highly skilled employees, it's not a bad idea. Nor is it a new idea. My father was still an employee at Morgan Construction Company when he died at seventy-two. In the 1800s in this country there was no such thing as retirement; people just kept working until they became too ill to work, or until they died. As Bink says, "Why retire?"

The benefits of not retiring are obvious. People continue working for financial reasons or because they love their work. Those in white-collar professions may find that the salary, based on many years of employment, keeps increasing. The prestige and sense of self-worth and security often continue. As the years of service increase, the vacations may lengthen, or extended unpaid time off may be possible. If your employer really wants you to stay, you might be able to arrange for flextime or a shorter work week. A person might be able to enjoy the benefits of retirement without actually retiring.

However, there are issues to think about. For any of several reasons, your employer might pressure you to step down. You will cost the company more each year if your salary increases. If you and your peers stay on for a decade, promotion opportunities will likely become limited for others in the organization. If you hold a leadership position, people may begin to wonder if the time has come for a new leadership style, a fresh vision, and higher energy: "If we had a younger pastor, we might attract young families to the church." The pressure to retire may also come from the family. Your spouse may want to spend more time with the grandchildren or move to a different climate. If you toss and turn at night because of a stressful job, it may be time to move on.

Some blue-collar workers at a factory like Morgan Construction Company find the physical requirements of the work harder to bear every year. There may be a less demanding position available in another department or company, but is the move worthwhile? Many workers I knew at Morgan's were eager to retire so that they could spend more energy and time on an avocation that was part of their calling. "Why retire?" It's a good question, but not always an easy one to answer.

Substitute Work

Some pastors who are great preachers and who miss writing a sermon every week want to continue that routine. Others like to preach the same sermon in different congregations. Either way, the reward can be immense: you get to do the task that is most meaningful without all those evening meetings. The same benefits may go with substitute teaching, nursing, or working on the floor of a department store during the Christmas rush.

The negative side of being the substitute teacher is that you don't know the students, you are not a peer of the faculty, and the students can be brutal with substitutes. The supply preacher has to win the confidence of a congregation every Sunday. I avoid the role of "guest minister." My best sermons came from the life of the congregation in the recent past; and I miss the conversation later in the week with someone who didn't agree with the sermon. I suppose the same is true for a chef or a desk clerk. Being a substitute is a different job from the one you held before retirement.

Part-time Work

Many enjoy a part-time position that comes with regular hours, as substituting generally does not. This is an excellent alternative when the pension is not sufficient, the previous employer forced you into early retirement, or you really want a trip to Europe. There are many part-time positions available, such as pastor of a very small congregation, minister of visitation of a large church, part-time secretary at a doctor's office, or member of the ski patrol at Aspen. When I asked Bink if he planned to work at Vertex forever, he said, "If not, I have enough contacts in the city to work as a consultant again."

Part-time employment helps with the family budget. In one sense, the part-time position delays retirement. Will the income and benefits of the part-time position be enough that you can delay drawing on your pension? If so, that is a big advantage, since when delayed, pension payments often are larger. Will the addition of the part-time salary along with the pension be adequate? If not, what will happen when work is no longer possible? If the answer is "no European trip," that's fine. But if it means no more health insurance, that's not good.

Interim Work

Most denominations recommend that after one pastor leaves and before a new pastor begins, the congregation be served by an interim pastor who can facilitate the change of leadership.

Congregations need time to grieve the loss of a beloved pastor or to correct a faulty system that prompted a change in leadership. An interim pastorate might be a full-time or a part-time position. In the secular world, the interim administrator, superintendent, supervisor, or long-term substitute helps the institution prepare for a new administration.

The interim position is different from that of the pastor, CEO, or educator. The person who specializes in saving bankrupt companies has skills that differ from those of an experienced CEO. The interim school superintendent or university president is not a short-term version of the permanent leader. The work of trained "intentional interim" pastors is very different from that of pastors who just keep the ship afloat until a new person is called. Serving as an "intentional interim" is a distinct occupation. Many spend whole careers traveling across the country to serve as interim pastors or CEOs. The role of the interim is also vital. The integrity of institutions depends on the skill of the interim leader. If the employees have not worked through the issues of the transition, the new executive will not succeed. If a retired pastor is interested in this task, excellent training is available. There is a real need for skilled interims.

Full- or Part-time Volunteers

I know people who are volunteer pastors in the church, and they are committed clergy. In some cases they serve tiny parishes in rural or urban settings, and their ministry makes a difference to the whole community. Some work full-time, some part-time; some preach at least once a month; others visit shut-ins, teach adult education classes, administer the business side of the church, or run the church school and youth groups. Lay volunteers are equally indispensable in every congregation I know, and they get no salary. All of us who worship in churches know how indebted we are to volunteers.

The same is true of every calling. When teachers retire, they often volunteer in the classroom or as tutors; "empty nesters" visit nursing homes or help nonprofit agencies; accountants volunteer as church treasurers. We can use what we learned in the past as a creative and important gift to others during our retirement years.

Something Different

As they retire, many of my friends center their lives outside the church. Many retired clergy belong to a congregation and attend regularly, but they are not focused on the parish ministry. They are grateful to have had many happy years as a pastor, but now they want something different, something they had always hoped to try, a hobby they intend to pursue seriously. Let me describe the ways some retired clergy I know have followed their calling outside parish ministry.

The Arts

Two of my friends are poets in retirement. Both wrote poetry as a hobby their entire adult lives, but now it *is* their life. The poet is who they are, what they have been given; and poetry is what they do full-time. Both introduce themselves as poets. George has worked on a book of poems that will be published soon. Roberta has written and published texts for hymns. Two other friends are musicians. Larry played the piano all his life and now sings in two choral groups. Kate is still a pastor, but the congregation has agreed that she needs to spend a large portion of her time composing. She has published many pieces already; imagine what she will do in retirement. One layperson learned landscape painting after he retired. He took a few lessons and poured himself into the new hobby. He says, "I haven't sold any of my work, but I see everything from a new perspective now."

These people aren't just playing around with their spare time; theirs is not a selfish life. They have a calling, a way of witnessing to the power and beauty of God—a ministry for both lay and ordained. Antonio Vivaldi, born in 1678 and ordained a priest in 1703, found within a year of being ordained that he no longer wished to celebrate mass. Supposedly he sometimes left the altar to jot down a musical idea in the sacristy.[4] He taught music at a home for orphaned, abandoned, and indigent children. Finally, music was his life—music that we value three centuries after Vivaldi's death. His calling included something different.

Academia

One of my friends earned a degree after retirement—a master's in history. That experience isn't at all unusual these days. Going back to school is what retirement is for. We who are retired are students in one classroom or another—elder hostels or a lifelong learning program at the local community college. Many of us are teachers in retirement. I continued teaching a course in seminary and, like many retired clergy, teach adult-education classes in our congregation.

Justice

Some don't apply for an existing occupation but invent a new way to engage the world. To clergy who have preached justice, retirement opens the possibility of devoting their lives to that high calling. The laity also ask how they can devote their retirement to this urgent call. What might we do in the name of justice? We could run for office or volunteer for a political party or campaign. We could work in a soup kitchen, a low-income housing agency, or an environmental advocacy group. Retirement can be an opportunity to do what we have never before had time to do.

Volunteerism

Many people volunteer outside the discipline they worked in before retiring. Volunteers are in demand at the local hospital, museum, public school, or social-service agency. One couple I know serve as ushers at Symphony Hall in Albuquerque. They regularly meet interesting people, hear great music, and enjoy a night out on the town.

Volunteering outside our own profession is an important piece of life. The friends we make at the hospital, museum, or school may widen our horizons, introducing us to new ideas and activities. For church people to volunteer only at church is to miss the fascinating people they can meet in other places. I would think one volunteer activity that is different from our usual routine keeps us growing.

A New Occupation

Since 1980 Jimmy Carter has been a model for us all. After he left the presidency, he created an institute that works for peace and justice in the world. That was his passion, his calling all his life; it became a full-time job in his retirement. None of us will travel to as many troubled places or make as much difference in the world as he, but if we follow our passion, our calling, what we do in retirement might well be as important as what we did before.

A public-school teacher Jackie and I met on a trip was retiring the following year. We spent time in buses, trains, and airports listening to her think aloud about what she might do in retirement. Her calling was teaching teenagers. Her gifts, her identity, her place in life centered on being a teacher in middle school. "Those kids don't know how to deal with money," she said. "They don't know how to earn, spend, save, or give money away." I will always remember the moment when something clicked in her—"That's what I should do in retirement: start a school of money management for teens." The trouble with traveling around the world is that you seldom see again those wonderful new friends you met on the tour bus. I wonder if she started that school!

Life in a Local Church

In most agencies, volunteers help to promote and finance the organization. The work that I look for involves volunteers at the center of the program. As a hospice volunteer I am assigned to a patient, along with a chaplain, a social worker, a home health aide, a nurse, and a "homemaker/companion." As a volunteer, I am asked to pay attention to the needs of the patient, and I am encouraged to contact team colleagues with the patient's concerns. The volunteer is at the center of the service to patient and family.

Volunteers are also the center of a congregation's ministry. Volunteers teach children and youth, visit the sick and needy, administer the business of the church, and lead worship. All of that is done with the pastor and the staff, but volunteers are at the center.

Lay volunteers are often amazed to learn that there aren't many rules that define their role in the church. The bylaws of the institution and the policies adopted by the board or committee responsible for each task are the only written guidelines. The definition of most of the ministry is worked out along the way. While that open-endedness can be a problem when one person insists on his or her preference, usually the flexibility is the genius of the system. It may be hard for new volunteers to know what exactly is expected of them as the new treasurer or official board member. But that is what's so exciting: the new volunteers may have some great ideas learned in other churches or in their careers. The longtime church workers may begin,

"We've always done it this way." The negotiation between the old way and the new results in a stronger set of assumptions, however. Sometimes the negotiation requires help from pastor or lay leaders; sometimes it fails, and the volunteer or parishioner is disappointed—and the failure is what people remember. But most of the time, in my experience, the negotiated definition of the volunteer's role is a miracle.

The same kind of creativity can arise when the pastor resigns or retires. There is one rule written into the ordination liturgy, into denominational documents on clergy ethics, and into the culture of congregations of nearly every tradition: When you resign from a church, really resign; when you retire from a pastorate, really retire. Bob Kemper puts it this way: "Look upon retirement as disordination. . . . No one is asking you to stop being a Christian, just stop being a pastor to that church and its people."[5] I think "disordination" is too strong, since we are still ordained in our retirement, but the word accurately indicates that we no longer have an ordained place in a church that we no longer serve as pastor.

That rule may seem harsh at first, but it is kind. Only if the former pastor really leaves will he or she be able to get on with the rest of life. This rule enables us seriously to consider the question, "What am I going to do with the rest of my life?" The rule is also kind to the congregation. It enables the church to get on with the next stage of its life with a new pastor. I don't mean that this rule is easy. It is hard to lose the pastoral relationship that has been so healing; it is hard to walk away from precious relationships and ministries. The resulting grief must be worked through in worship and congregational life, in the hearts of everyone in the congregation, and in the pastor. This rule enables us to get beyond grief to newness of life. When this rule is broken, the church and the retired pastor suffer greatly.

Having said that, I think that everything else has to be worked out along the way. The retiring pastor has to be in conversation with the board and the staff of the church. This conversation has to be filled with respect and blunt honesty. A rule for every possible situation is not feasible. What is right and fair for a suburban church in New England won't necessarily work for a rural parish in Montana. Making up the rules as we go means that we can make decisions relevant to the specific context and the personalities involved. But deciding what is right isn't easy. Let me give you some examples.

When the pastor resigns, should she or he come back for a baptism, wedding, or funeral? Remembering the established rule, it seems there is no way that the retired pastor should return. Yet there could be an exception. Suppose the bride is the retired pastor's daughter or grandchild who is still a member of that church. Suppose the funeral is for the organist who served with the retired pastor for ten years. Sometimes life isn't simple.

The retired pastor who has really retired will have established a tradition of not returning, because if you officiate at one funeral, you will have to do so for all. But what if the new pastor really wants his predecessor to return? What if the bride's family is the largest contributor and a close friend of the retired pastor? Will either pastor have any choice? Of course they will. The retired pastor could explain to the family that the new pastor doesn't stand a chance if the retired minister keeps presiding at the weddings of his old friends. If that doesn't persuade folks, the new pastor can explain that the wedding involves several conversations before the wedding as well as ministry to the couple and the families after the service, so the new pastor needs to be intimately involved in the whole ministry. If a compromise is required, the new pastor might offer to invite the retired pastor to take part in the service. An honest and sensitive conversation with everyone involved is the way to work things out along the way, and the principles will have been forcefully explained, even if a compromise is required.

Should the retired clergy and family continue to live in the same town after retiring? The answer to that question has been clear in my mind since meeting with Bob Kemper when I was fifty: If I stay in the neighborhood, I will have to keep my mouth shut about what is happening in the church I used to serve. Since I could never do that, I moved far enough away that I wouldn't know what was going on in the parish. But others own their home or are disciplined enough to keep their opinions to themselves. Everyone has to work it out. Retired and new pastors need to have a polite but brutally honest conversation. Both clergy need to explain their position to the congregation before and after the transition.

Should the retired pastor continue as a member of a former congregation? Again, it may be hard to imagine moving from the pulpit to the pew of the same congregation. But it can work and may even be necessary in some situations. In some small towns in rural America there is no other church to join; there are urban churches that are large and strong enough to absorb the retired clergy family. Again, it has to be worked out. One pastor I know told the retiring pastor and the congregation that she would welcome him back to active church membership when she was fully accepted by the church. She then listed several achievements, like a balanced budget and an increase in membership, that would be evidence that she was really accepted.

Most of us move our membership to a new parish after retirement. The question is, what should our role be as a retired pastor in that new congregation? At the pastor's invitation, some share leadership with the pastor, visiting the sick, teaching an adult class, or preaching occasionally. Others want none of that and are simply cheerleaders. Should retired clergy serve on committees of the church? What happens when there is a change in pastoral leadership? Should retired clergy serve on the search committee; should they nominate candidates; should they be in conversation with the placement officer of the judicatory? My answer is again, work it out. No rule will work for every church, and the congregation and the clergy have to settle issues as they come up.

What happens if it doesn't work out? What if communication breaks down? How do we manage the anger that can come from an inability to find a way forward? The answer may be a judicatory staff person—for my denomination, the associate conference minister (ACM). The ACM is pastor to clergy, retired clergy, and congregations. If the new pastor and the retiring pastor can't come to an agreement, the ACM will try to bring them together. Everyone can be sure that the judicatory official will work hard to reconcile differences before they escalate to schism.

The Road Not Taken

When I was fifty, I went to a career-counseling center to see if it was time for me to leave the parish ministry and try my hand at something different. I wondered whether I should apply for a position in the regional conference, the mission board of the national church, or a seminary. It was a wonderful week of reflection that resulted in a new commitment to parish ministry. Only in looking back on that experience did a striking insight become clear. Those three alternatives that I rejected in my midlife quest—ministry in a conference, global missions, and a theological seminary—became the options I embraced in my retirement.

Having come from a family that has lived in New England since 1633, I find that the poet of New England, Robert Frost, speaks my language when he describes the choice made when two paths diverge in the woods. Retirement gives us a chance to explore "the road not taken."

For Reflection

- Where do you see yourself in early retirement—keeping on within the church or pursuing something different?

- What specific options within each category might interest you?
- If you were to create your own part-time or volunteer position, what characteristics would it have?
- In retirement, what do you imagine will be your place within a congregation?

CHAPTER 6

It's Not
All About
Me

I have described how our calling gives us meaning, fulfillment, and access to a community. In this chapter I want to be clear that our calling is not only about our own lives. Our calling—which includes our identity, gifts, and occupation—is dedicated to a purpose that transcends our personal agenda. It's not all about me.

Legend of Survival

Two Old Women: An Alaska Legend of Betrayal, Courage, and Survival is an account passed from generation to generation in the oral tradition. Alaskan author Velma Wallis wrote it down so that we could all know of it. It tells the story of an Athabaskan tribe in the days before Western culture touched the banks of the Yukon, Porcupine, and Tanana rivers. "The People" is the name of this band of nomads. The People were near starvation, and winter lay before them. Terror led the chief to make the hard decision.

"We are going to have to leave the old ones behind." His eyes quickly scanned the crowd for reactions. But the hunger and

cold had taken their toll, and The People did not seem to be
shocked. . . . In those days, leaving the old behind in times of
starvation was not an unknown act. . . . The starkness of the
primitive land seemed to demand it.[1]

The two women left behind didn't sit waiting for death from
the freezing wind. They plodded on, day after day, toward a
place by the river that they remembered from the old days. The
legend relates how they survived the trek through the winter,
how they caught and dried fish and meat through the summer,
and how they hunkered down, ready for another winter.

Meanwhile, the People did not manage the winter as well
as the women. The People seemed to give up trying to survive.
In the fall, the chief returned to the place where they had left
the old women. Why? Even he didn't know. When he reached
the place, there was no evidence—no bone, no shred of the
tent or blanket that the People had left with the women. An
experienced guide whispered to the chief, "Maybe they moved
on."[2] The chief ordered long-distance runners to search for the
two women. The search party found the remains of the first
campground used by the two women, and the second. After
passing many more remains of campfires, they came to a place
where they could smell the smoke of a fire. At first the women
didn't trust the People; they were afraid they would be left behind
again. Then the women said to each other, "If they do the same
to us again, we will survive [again]."[3] In that confidence, the
women made their presence known and encouraged the People
to stay for the winter near the women's camp. "A well-trodden
path lay between the two camps."[4] These two women saved the
People from starvation, not only with their dried fish but with
their exceptional courage.

"How could they have left the elderly behind?" is the first
question people ask about the legend. Most of us *choose* to retire
and leave the office, classroom, or parish behind. Still, some

retired people feel that they have been forced to retire—by poor health, corporate reorganization, or other factors beyond their control. Whether we retire by choice or not, we find, after we've left the job, that gradually we no longer hear from former colleagues or institutions. Contact information is deleted from directories. It seems that we are now out of the loop. But in truth, the congregation or colleagues we left behind may feel that *we* abandoned *them*. The issue is not who abandoned whom, but what we can do when there has been a parting of the ways. The legend tells us that the two women refused to sit and wait for death. They decided to live. The legend addresses those who feel they have been left behind, saying, "Don't sit there waiting to die. Move on with your life."

For me, the point of the legend is this: "It's not all about me." The People went on, focused on their own issues; they went on toward death. Children died of hunger, and the spirit that had kept the People together slipped away. The community gave up trying. The women were committed to each other. Neither of them could have managed alone. Each struggled on, not only for herself but also for her soul mate. Only in the end did they realize that by their devotion to one another and by their courage to carry on day by day, they were able to rescue the People. The courage of these two women allowed them, at the end of the legend, to save the tribe that had forsaken them.

Throughout life we may continue our trek day by day without seeing the remarkable results of our endeavors. We may struggle on, for our own sake or for the sake of our partner, without realizing that we are engaged in a noble calling. If we are true to that calling, if we persist, we will have contributed to the survival of the whole community. It is to be hoped that we will recognize the magnitude of that effort when we reflect on our story, that we will see see that God was there in our struggle and understand that our calling is not just "about me." It is about the whole of God's creation.

Passion

When we are searching for our role in God's creation, we may hear people say, "Follow your passion." That is good advice, but what does it mean? Much of life is directed by what we believe—our doctrinal, ideological, and theological assumptions. That is fine as far as those ideas can carry us, but following our passion is another motivating piece of life. Passion is a powerful emotion. Most people associate passion with sexuality. It is that and more. To be passionate is to be so driven by intense love that we feel boundless in our enthusiasm and devotion. Passion adds feeling to our beliefs and commitments.

To be passionate is not only to focus on ourselves and our appetites but also to be committed to another. Passion is not only how we feel; it is also about the object of our devotion. Passion is to live and die for another. It's not just about me; it's about me and what or whom I am passionate about. Passion is our ardent love and the object of our devotion.

Passion can be a positive or a negative force in our lives, depending on the object of our devotion. On the one hand, the object of our love often pulls us out of ourselves into the passionate life. We claim our passion, and at the same time we are drawn into this commitment. On the other hand, some people are passionate about themselves—their wealth, fame, or power. If we are passionately in love with ourselves, we create a short circuit; such passion is demonic. The object of our passion marks the difference between idolatry and faithfulness.

It was hard for Roger to retire as a firefighter. The ability to stand in the chaos and find a way back to an ordered life was his passion. Out of that commitment, he brought people out of death and into life. It was hard for him to leave that passion behind. Every time Jackie had to decide to go this way rather than that, she felt drawn by something beyond herself. The decision to become a teacher, to go to Turkey as a missionary, to get married, to stay at home with the children, to get a doctorate—in every case she was drawn: "I felt it was the right thing for me to do." The first time Bink used the word "call" in my interview with him, he was talking about the CEO at Vertex who said, "I know you love what you're doing, but if I'm successful, I'm going to save about a million lives." Bink explained, "That was the call that I had to answer, and I am so glad that I did." He was drawn by the magnitude of the pharmaceuticals industry. The passion behind my own call was the power of the church to support me in my stuttering failures and to challenge me with new possibilities in Massachusetts and in the global ministries of the wider church.

Consider the passion of the two old women in the legend Velma Wallis recounts. Their journey from death to life was energized by passion alone. They were powered by a love of life, a passion for each other. Their determination was fueled by anger at the People, the memory of a lovely camp on a river filled with fish, a self-confidence that they could face an Alaskan winter and survive.

An important ingredient of the women's journey was their saving the very people who had left them behind, although they didn't know that was their purpose until the pilgrimage was over. I know many people who live remarkable lives that constitute a noble example for us all, and they don't see their nobility at all. Like the two old women, they just trudge along. Often, it is only in the end that we see, and with any luck, in the end they will also see the amazing courage of their lives.

Most of the saints I know feel they don't have the luxury of living what they consider a worthwhile life. They would like to be artists, or organists, or teachers, or biblical scholars, but they don't think they have the money or the time or even a clear understanding of what it is they long to be. So they stumble on, just trying to make a living. They never see that sainthood is the courage to keep on keeping on, even when they don't know where

God will lead them. Saving a million lives isn't accomplished only in the pharmaceuticals industry. The stumbles for which these people apologize constitute a courageous witness that will inspire family and friends, to the second and third generation, not to give up.

The passion narrative in the Bible is the story of Jesus in those last days of his life. He struggled on to the temple, to the upper room, to Pilate's inquisition, to solitary prayer in the night, to death on the cross. Sometimes he seemed to understand God's ability to turn the crucifixion into an Easter; sometimes he didn't see that at all: "My God, my God why have you forsaken me?" (Matt. 27:46). Passion doesn't require money or free time or even a clear understanding about what God is doing. Passion is love lived out with integrity and gentleness; passion is love focused on the other—on God, on neighbor.

Mount Pisgah

The Bible is full of stories about people who were passionate—sometimes about the right things, sometimes not. Listen to Moses, one of the Bible's most passionate figures, speaking to those who had followed him out of Egypt and through the wilderness. Moses is explaining to the people what he learned from God:

> At that time . . . I entreated the LORD, saying: "O Lord GOD, you have only begun to show your servant your greatness and your might; what god in heaven or on earth can perform deeds and mighty acts like yours! Let me cross over to see the good land beyond the Jordan, that good hill country and the Lebanon." But the LORD was angry with me on your account and would not heed me. The LORD said to me, "Enough from you! Never speak to me of this matter again! Go up to the top of Pisgah and look around you to the west, to the north, to the south, and to

the east. Look well, for you shall not cross over this Jordan. But charge Joshua, and encourage and strengthen him, because it is he who shall cross over at the head of this people and who shall secure their possession of the land that you will see."

Deuteronomy 3:23-28

"Enough from you!" God said. "Never speak to me of this matter again." Why was God so angry? Moses wanted to lead Israel across the Jordan River into the Promised Land. God believed that if Joshua was going to succeed in the new land, he needed a role in the exodus from slavery. He, not Moses, needed to "cross over at the head of this people." God was angry at Moses because Moses assumed that the whole miraculous journey to the Promised Land was about him—his leadership, his courage, his faithfulness. For the sake of the people of Israel, so that Joshua would be a leader they knew and trusted in the dangerous new land, God said that Moses would not cross over the Jordan.

God was the one to confront the Pharaoh; God delivered the Ten Commandments at Mount Sinai; God provided bread every morning when there was no food. God did all of that through Moses. At the foot of Mount Pisgah, Moses came to realize that this calling wasn't just about him. There was room for more than one leader. Pisgah's message is true for everyone who feels called by God. The object of our passion is so huge that it requires a community of people, not just me.

Moses also learned at the foot of Mount Pisgah that our calling often ends before the job is finished. When we are not able to carry on to the end, we shouldn't be surprised. That is the result of a passion for someone or something that is huge—bigger than what we can do in our lifetime. It was his ego that enabled Moses to lead Israel through the wilderness, and it was his ego that made him want to lead all the way over the Jordan. Is it our ego that brought us this far and that makes us want to lead forever? It was Moses's ego that angered God. Moses teaches us that our calling often ends before the tasks are finished.

Perhaps the most important and surprising lesson comes from this command of God's: "Charge Joshua, and encourage and strengthen him, because it is he who shall cross over at the head of this people." Not only was Moses not going to finish the task; he was to train his successor. Part of the calling was passing this call on to Joshua. "Charge," "encourage," and "strengthen" were the verbs God used in describing this call to Moses. Supporting Joshua in his call to carry on the leadership of Israel was the final ingredient of the calling of Moses that began at the burning bush. Moses didn't choose his successor—God did that. But Moses needed to affirm that choice and make it work. It's not enough to resign and stay out of our successor's way. We need to "charge, encourage, and strengthen" our successors. Every time we sneer at our successors, thinking that their failure shows our success, we can expect God to be angry at us and our egotistical assumptions. From Moses we learn that part of the call we have enjoyed all these decades is the charge to make certain the next generation of leaders is better than the last.

Our calling isn't just about us. It is God's call, not something we invented. It's the object of our passion that shaped us, not just our preference. The mark of our success is not our satisfaction. It is the courage to struggle on as Jesus did in the last days of his life. Sometimes that seems to be a blow to our ego, but most of the time we understand this truth to be good news indeed: "It's not all about me."

For Reflection

- In retrospect, the two women understood that they had saved the People. Looking back on life, what is the larger benefit of your calling?
- What is your passion? How were you drawn into it? What is the object of your devotion?

- If God were to say to you as he said to Moses, "charge, encourage, and strengthen," what would that mean to you?
- Can your passion be reflected in who you are as well as what you do?

CHAPTER 7

Don't Just
Do Something,
Stand There

In many cultures one's place in the world is defined by lineage, marriage, or place of residence. In our culture we are measured by what we do. That is why retirement is so difficult. We are afraid that when we no longer have a job, we will no longer be someone of worth, stature, or significance. That was Kim's concern about retirement. In this book, I have suggested that our calling is still in effect during retirement. Our life's plan is to do something for others, for the world, for God—that is, we plan to serve, with or without a salary, until we die.

But what happens when we are no longer able to work? The hard fact of life is that most of us will not be able to work until we die. My predecessor in my last parish died in his nineties on a Saturday night as he was writing a sermon for Sunday. His body was found slumped over the desk. That is unusual! Most of us will die after an illness. We can try to avoid life-threatening sickness by watching our diet, avoiding addictions, and exercising. But still, we will probably not die writing tomorrow's sermon. That means that we who want to die "with our boots on" might see the day when we are no longer be able to care for ourselves. Someone else might have to change his or her work pattern to care for us, or we might have to give up our own work to care for a loved one.

In this book I maintain that we are called for life. It is clear how our calling can be still in force during retirement, but are we called if we are no longer able to *do* anything?

Called to Be

We are called not only to *do* God's work in the world, but also to *be* God's people in the world. Consider again the definition of our calling. In our working and our retirement years, our occupation is *what we do*. Our call to do God's work in the world is a blessed calling. It is not only leading the congregation, or teaching the class, or keeping the books; it is nurturing our child, loving our spouse; it is doing the right thing. To do what we are called to do takes courage, imagination, faith, and commitment. But our identity is *who we are*. We are also called to *be* the person God intends us to be. That identity is marked by integrity rather than greed, care for others rather than self-absorption, humility rather than arrogance. Our gifts are seen in the way we grow as human beings and in the way we carry out our occupation.

Our calling includes both doing and being; the two are connected. A teacher gets the subject matter across to the students in first grade because she knows what she is talking about, and she speaks a language the children understand; she does her job well. She succeeds also because she is a person the students know, admire, and respect; they want to learn because of who she is. A wonderfully personable executive in business can fail because of incompetence (what he does), and a skillful executive can fail because of arrogance (who he is). How many times have we heard a parishioner say, "He doesn't preach very well, he lacks administrative skills, and often he doesn't know what to say in a tragic moment, but he's a wonderful pastor"? Such a parishioner loves her pastor not for what he does but for who he is. Our occupation and our identity, our doing and our being, are connected.

The Transparent Life: Being and Doing

As a pastor I came to feel that the people in the congregation were able to see right through me. They recognized my shy side, my impatient eagerness to get on with life, my weariness with never-ending committee meetings. That meant I couldn't get away with anything. Because I was open with them, they felt free to be open with me: "Paul, what you said in the sermon this morning didn't match with what you said at the party last week." That appeared to be an occupational hazard until I retired. Now I see that transparency is universal. People notice when a neighbor does one thing but represents himself as a person who would never do such a thing. Some people don't like to be so transparent; they pull down the shades of their lives, hoping for privacy. But people see right through the drawn blinds to the truth. Who we are shows on our faces, in the way we stand, or in our unintended sigh. This transparency, which allows others to see through our weakness to the essence of who we are, is our witness; our very being is revealed through what we do.

Elisabeth Kübler-Ross, author of *On Death and Dying,* and David Kessler, an end-of-life specialist and leader in the field of hospice care, say, "This generation knows how to *do,* but doesn't always know how to *be.*"[1] Decades after I graduated from Middlebury, I told D. K. Smith how he had helped me decide to be a parish minister. It was because I believed he was a great human being that his sparsely furnished home convinced me that a large salary wasn't a reason to choose a career. He didn't know what I was talking about, because what influenced me wasn't anything he *did* for me. What moved me was what he believed about money, what motivated him to be a professor—*who he was.*

In the 1920s the mission board of my denomination decided to give up "doing mission work" in Turkey and decided to *be* that mission. The mission faced dramatic circumstances and choices. The Ottoman Empire was on the losing side of World War I. The European powers divided Turkey up among the victors—this section to England, that to France, another to Greece. A popular general, Mustafa Kemal Atatürk, created an army that succeeded in establishing the Turkish Republic. He then turned the country toward the Western world. Men would no longer wear the fez, women would not cover their heads, the language would use Western script, women would have all the rights enjoyed by men, and religion and government would be definitely separate. No school was to teach Islam, and likewise no mission school would be permitted to teach Christianity. With the end of the war, most Greek and Armenian people who had been served by the mission during the Ottoman Empire left Turkey; and in the new Turkish Republic missionaries would no longer be allowed to teach the Christian faith to Turkish students. The mission board members debated: should we close the mission in Turkey and focus on countries that welcome us, or should we stay in Turkey, even though we have to obey the law and not teach the faith?

The board decided to ask the missionaries to stay in Turkey and let their presence be the witness. The mission work continued in four schools that prepared students for universities; two clinics; a hospital. and the Red House Press, which published Turkish-English dictionaries, books on the environment, and children's books. All of that was noble work; these were important services to render. But the missionaries were not allowed to teach the gospel, which had been the essence of the mission. The board's intention was for the missionaries to *be with* the Muslim people and to be as transparent as possible, so that by being there, they would reveal who they were and why they were in Turkey. The way the principal shared her power with staff and students, the way a teacher treated a student's misbehavior, the outreach to poor people in neighboring villages—all of that was the witness.

At annual meetings of the mission and in the evaluation back in the Boston office of the American Board there was an intentional focus on the witness. While three missionaries are still there, the Turkey mission has been turned over to graduates of the mission schools, who formed an indigenous Turkish agency to run the institutions. Jackie and I stay in touch with alumnae of the schools and still hear them say that what the schools miss most is the missionary presence. Graduates of the schools talk about the remarkably generous actions of the missionaries. It seems that the missionaries have grown in stature since their death.

Noble as that mission in Turkey was, it would have made a more powerful witness if doing and being could have supported one another. It would have been more successful if power sharing could have been connected to the power of Jesus on the cross, if forgiveness offered could have been linked to the mercy of the father who welcomed the prodigal home, if the service to the poor could have been tied to the priority to help the impover-ished that is found in both Christianity and Islam.

Still, even at the time, many missionaries thought the mis-sion was strengthened when people could not justify their pres-ence by offering a class on biblical studies; instead they had to concentrate on living the Christian life. Being limited to just being there seemed a defeat to some American critics, but "liv-ing the Christian life" is probably the best mission imaginable. If we were limited to living the Christian life in our churches, we might be more successful in our witness.

The Power of Being

At the beginning of this chapter a question was posed: "It is clear how our calling can be still in force during retirement, but are we called if we are no longer able to *do* anything?" Imagine what it is like for George, a retiree who is recovering from a cerebral hemorrhage. His whole life is dedicated to rehabilitation. He spends hours at the gym, hours working with several therapists, hours exercising on the living-room floor. Doing everything possible to recover is a full-time job for George. But how is this effort related to his calling?

The answer is that George is called to be a witness. As D. K. Smith freed me to consider ordination by who he was, so George's persistent optimism that he will recover is an inspiration to us all. As people are able to see the courage it takes for the pastor to cope with the conflicts and troubles of the congregation, so we are able to see how brave George is to be so patient. As the missionaries to Turkey recognized the power of living the Christian life only when they were not allowed to teach the faith, so we who are not able to do much of anything are still called to be witnesses to the healing power of God.

Profound illness can provide an opportunity to deal with who we are. When someone is seriously ill, the whole family—the one who is sick, the spouse, the siblings, and the caregivers—is affected. This circumstance is a pivotal moment in the life of this family. We have all seen parents divorce after the agony of a child's illness and death. We have also seen family members become clear about their calling as a result of their grief. I don't have a simple answer to explain why one family fails and the other grows from the sorrow. I do believe, however, that the witness of courage and faith is an important ingredient for growth. There isn't much we can do to lighten the burden, but there are important ways we can help one another by being who we are in the face of illness and death.

Our call to *be* is particularly important in the midst of stress. When someone is ill at home, it seems that we have time only to endure the laundry, meds, meals, and transportation. I maintain that this is the moment when we need to *be*. We need to be with the patient, to listen to how she feels and what she thinks—not as a patient but as a person. This is the time to be not only with the patient, but also with the children, the extended family, and ourselves.

When we are no longer able to "fix things," it is time for us to center on who we are called to be. In fact, I believe that *being* is more important in a crisis than *doing*. My call to parish ministry was a result of who D. K. Smith was. Turkish missionaries are remembered for the Christian life they lived. Grief is turned to growth when we can see into the depths of who we are.

Nurturing Ourselves

If our "call to be" is so important, how can we nurture the "being" side of our calling? How can we grow in our inner stature? I believe that we grow through reflection. "Theological reflection" was the term used for supervision of the theology students who worked with us in the church. Supervisors were to focus not only on what the students did, but also on who they were. It was important that they treated young people, disabled people, and elderly people well, but of more significance was who they were for the congregation. They needed to grow to a point of maturity at which they were able to understand themselves as ministers, followers of Jesus, witnesses of the gospel. My question is this: "How do we do theological reflection in our retirement?"

Jackie and I spent three winters writing a family history. It was an exploration into the influence our parents had on us, and that their parents had on them, and a hard look at the life we shared as a couple and as a family. Our purpose was to write some of these family stories for future sons-in-law and daughters-in-law so that they could see something of the family into which they were marrying. But in the process we developed a new understanding of who we are. For me it was a realization that the handicaps of childhood still linger in me, that what I keep finding is not a way to fix them but a way to go around them. For Jackie it was a realization that her struggles to adjust had sometimes overpowered her inherent biculturalism.

Others reflect on their lives by going back to school. During the years at Middlebury, professors kept telling us that a liberal education was not only a strategy for getting a job; it was also an opportunity to become a better human being. None of us believed that for a moment. In retirement, I am struck by how many of us have come around to that insight. We hunger for a learning environment—elder hostels, classes at the local college, workshops on computer science, a course in history, or instruction in a new language. Now that we don't have to think about our resume, we are free to learn in order to become a more complete human being.

For me, learning is a search for mentors to help me understand who I am, and history has become a rich source for me. Three books about three U.S. presidents illustrate my search. I read *My Life* by Bill Clinton[2] when President George W. Bush was insisting that no mistakes had been made in Iraq. In his book President Clinton acknowledged mistake after mistake. That openness is a model for me: we learn from our mistakes only if we acknowledge them. *Team of Rivals* by Doris Kearns Goodwin[3] is full of examples from Lincoln's tenure as president. He brought into his cabinet the people who had been his rivals for the nomination. It takes a mature, self-confident person to engage in that kind of teamwork. *John Adams* by David McCullough[4] was overwhelming for me. Adams was a New Englander, a Bostonian, and on every page I saw myself in him. He served overseas as an ambassador several times, but each assignment was a failure until his wife, Abigail, joined him. *Then* he succeeded. (I had been a little hesitant to tell people about Jackie's magic until I read about Abigail.) We stretch, deepen, and recognize who we are when we study people who have gone before us.

The call to *be* is a lifelong experience. We are often so caught up in what we are doing that we fail to notice who we have become. If we could have recognized the power of our identity over every occupation we inhabited, we would have been more complete and effective people.

Carl Perkins, a rabbi colleague of mine, says that when he was in seminary and assigned to serve as chaplain at a hospital, his supervisor said, "Don't just do something—stand there." That admonition describes the point of this chapter perfectly. What we do is important; our activity can be a blessing to the world in which we live. But arranging the pillow or checking the meds is not the chaplain's role; the chaplain needs just to *be there*—to listen, understand, and reflect. Being there is also a ministry to which we are called.

For Reflection

- Who are you? (Don't include what you *do* in the answer.)
- Do you think it might be harder to be a missionary if you were not permitted to teach a Bible class?
- In your retirement how will you reflect on the life you've lived?
- Write your memories of being a caregiver or a patient.
- How well will your "being" be expressed through illness and even death?

CHAPTER 8

The
Final
Call

"'I am the Alpha and the Omega,' says the Lord God, who is and who was and who is to come" (Rev. 1:8). God is always with us and is most recognizable in the beginning and at the end of life. The call at the end of life is our Omega. Being called for life includes our dying. I am convinced that newness of life for the family and for the terminally ill person is most powerfully present at the end of life. To speak of death is not a depressing endeavor; it is to explore still another expression of our calling.

Terminal Illness

To a large extent, we don't have a choice in how we die. The final call is given, not chosen. For Mildred, my mother, death came slowly, quietly, gently. Her mental sharpness departed before the pain arrived; it almost seemed to me that the fog that surrounded her consciousness was a blessing. For Lynda, Jackie's mother, the diagnosis was a public and dramatic event. On Monday evening in the hospital we got the bad news: "The cancer has metastasized into the lung, and there is nothing we can do." By the time we visited her the next afternoon, six pastors had been in the hospital to see her. For Jack, Jackie's father, the dementia marched on well ahead of death. His dying was quiet and sad. Leah, my aunt, died in her sleep in her eightieth year; the bedsheet was not disturbed.

Death is not the same for everyone. When life's end is near, our response is unique as well. Leah's last days were different from her sister Mildred's. But most of all our response to terminal illness is shaped by the way we have coped with every other crisis in life; we die the way we lived.

Mildred was a quiet, passive woman. She never complained, always waited for someone else to take the lead, never showed anger or frustration. She accepted whatever came in life and death and often went out of her way for the sake of others. Jackie and I had planned a trip to China, where our daughter was studying, and we invited my seventy-nine-year-old Aunt Lois to come with us. Mildred lingered on in the nursing home, and Lois wouldn't leave her sister's side. Two weeks before our departure, Mildred died, and Lois joined us in China. Everyone said that was typical of Mildred; she even died at a time that was convenient for others.

Lynda said, "Paul, I asked all six pastors the same question. 'I am scheduled for cataract surgery in a month. Now that we know I soon won't need my eyes, is it ethical for me to keep that appointment?'" I said, "We should live all the way until we die; I say, keep the appointment for the operation." "Good," she said. "You agree with the other six, and you all agree with me. I'll do it." She faced death the way she had faced every other challenge in life, accepting what she could not change and determined to respond in her own way. She accepted the fact that the cancer meant she was never strong enough for the eye surgery, but she never let poor eyesight interfere with life.

After his wife died, Jack moved to Indiana to live with his son and daughter-in-law. He suffered from dementia, but there was nothing passive about him. After the move, he took back the name given by his parents. After being Jack for his entire adulthood, he died as he was born, with the name Everett. The automobile had been his vehicle for mission; it was the way he helped others. He drove the school car in Izmir and on school trips around Turkey and Europe. In his retirement he drove children to a state prison to visit their mothers. He drove to grocery stores, gathered day-old-bread, and delivered it to the food pantry. And he drove across the United States to family reunions he had organized, so that all fourteen children and grandchildren could be together. It was a terrible moment when he had to relinquish his car keys. Months later he kept asking if he could have the keys back for just a short spin around the block. He died quietly in the nursing home.

Leah had no opportunity to respond to a diagnosis. Most of us envy her sudden death—no anguish, no nursing home, no longing for the car keys! While our preference is natural, we have limited control over the way we die. All the people in this list of deaths in the family took excellent care of themselves. Whether we are surprised by quick death or finally released from a long illness is not for us to determine. But how we respond is up to us.

Some people ask if that need be so. When the diagnosis is grim, why not choose suicide as a quick, painless way out of this life? In her novel *The Reckoning* May Sarton describes the last days of a woman named Laura, whose doctor had given her a prognosis of two years to live.

> She needed to get home as fast as possible. She started off, swinging out into the street so quickly a passing taxi nearly hit her. "In your own way, Laura, you idiot!" she said out loud. "Sudden death on Marlboro Street would never do."[1]

Right there, on the first page of the novel, May Sarton has defined the response. "In your own way" is a slogan Laura repeated often. That's the right way to respond, of course. The way we have lived is the right way to respond to death's approach. For Laura, jumping under the wheel of a taxi on Marlboro Street to escape, quit, run away, was not an option. To leave family without a farewell gesture of love wasn't her way.

Would we rather die without warning as Leah did? Perhaps, but the last days of life are important, with loved ones nearby to say good-bye. Perhaps there's something to learn in the anguish of terminal illness. Elisabeth Kübler-Ross put it this way:

> We all live with the possibility of death, but the dying live with the probability. What do they do with that heightened aware-ness? They take more risks because they haven't anything to lose anymore. Patients at the edge of life will tell you that they find incredible happiness in realizing that there is nothing to fear, nothing to lose.[2]

The whole meaning of life often becomes clear right at the end. I don't want to miss that.

The Continuity of Living and Dying

Our calling in the last years and months of life is related to the calling of all our previous years. Each phase of our individual call led to another stage and another, and this last experience flows out of the calling we have known all along the way.

Some months before Jack died, he was in a Friends nursing home in Indiana. Jackie went out to visit and found him dis-tressed. He fretted to her, "What am I supposed to be doing?" In a meeting of family and staff members, the question was asked, "How can we help him?" Together they came up with a theory. As a missionary and in retirement, Jack had always lived and worked for others. Here in the nursing home, everyone was taking care of him. The plan was to ask him to deliver mail to residents' rooms. Now, he was not always thinking straight at this point in his life, so a staff member followed him to make sure the right envelope went to the right patient, but it worked. He seemed much happier and calmer with a task that would allow him to continue his calling as missionary and minister. That meeting of staff and family gave him a peaceful last few weeks, because what he was, was reflected in what he did.

In her nursing home Mildred seemed very quiet, almost withdrawn. She and I had a precious relationship. During one visit I sat with her for a couple of hours. Well into my visit she mumbled something about a dream she had quite often. I asked a few questions, and the story unfolded. She dreamed that she was in an elevator lying on a hospital bed. When the door closed, the tube of the catheter was caught in the door as the elevator descended. Afraid she would be hurt, she pulled out the catheter. When she awoke, the nurse was angry, scolding: "Mildred, you pulled out the catheter again." She didn't argue or explain the dream, because to go along and not be a bother to people was her calling, the way she lived with her family and friends. She was embarrassed and ashamed that she kept irritating the staff. Of course, the nurses found a way to solve the problem when I described the dream to them.

When doctors told Lynda she had only six months to live, she made a list of things that she needed to do. She dispersed Turkish rugs and other treasures to various members of the family, arranged for someone to finish the biography of a once-famous Turkish woman she had begun writing decades before, planned her funeral service, arranged for her body to be given to a medical school for research, and answered every letter that came from around the world. She did it all by inspiring friends and family members, all of whom were happy to help.

The biggest task was what she called her program of reconciliation. This was the winter of 1989, and May Sarton had written *A Reckoning* in 1978. We don't know that Lynda read *A*

Reckoning, but it does appear that she applied the novel to her life. In the book Laura was determined to make peace before she died with her sisters, son, daughter, and mother, and with her best friend, who lived in England. In 1989, Lynda expanded that agenda to include everyone who she thought had ever had a problem with her. She asked each of these people who could to come and see her so that the two of them could reach reconciliation. We don't know the content of any of these conversations except two. One was the talk with our son, her grandson. He described his meeting with his grandmother in a touching story that he told in place of the sermon at the church of which he was a member in Red Lodge, Montana.

> Commanding the direction of the conversation as usual, she began, "John, you know I've always been fond of you." Then she told me about 1972, when she and Jack had returned from Turkey in retirement. She had been concerned, because she felt I was pulling back from them. It was a shocking moment, to hear Lynda Blake speak on an emotional level, to have her even hint that she'd felt rejected and hurt . . .
>
> "You're exactly right," I told her.
>
> I understood that she was settling up accounts while she still had the strength to do so. She was giving us honest evaluations, expecting the same in return. So I told her about my difficulties incorporating her into my young life. I said that she had eventually won me over. She smiled.[3]

We learned about the other conversation from Lynda herself. She and the conference minister had argued bitterly and publicly at an annual meeting some years before. The issue was the relationship between the Armenian community and the Turkish Republic. She told him that her purpose was to find reconciliation with him before she died, but he continued the debate. After he left, she mused, "I need to try to make peace with all;

but if some can't find it within themselves to be at peace with me, that doesn't mean I have failed."

The enormous length of her list of things to do was a challenge, since she was literally running out of time. What amazed me was her readiness to take the next step as it presented itself. Given her gifts for facing challenges and carrying on through adversity, she didn't have an alternative, but for her to take a step toward death with grace was remarkable. She played the piano for the last time; then soon after, she was not able to leave her bed, and she left the list of chores in the hands of others. I admired her courage.

Living in Turkey before e-mail, Lynda lived for the mail delivery. She had relied on the mail to stay in touch with family, friends, and directions from the home base. Throughout her life and especially in these last weeks, the mail delivery continued to be a big event in her day. Two days before she died, Jackie said, "Here's the mail, Mother." Lynda answered, "I don't want to read the mail anymore. It ties me too firmly to earth." Those words made it clear that she was near the last step. Her ability to surrender at each stage of her illness gave us all a glimpse of her person, her faith, her innermost being. She understood what she could manage, and that was a very large agenda, even as she was dying. But she was equally clear about what was out of her control. A few days before she died, she said, "I began this life with God by the River Spree, and I will end it with God, in God's own time."

I said in an earlier chapter that our calling is not an individual effort. We need community to discern, to understand, and to live our calling. The same is true of our dying. Laura, in May Sarton's novel, thought she could die her way and do it alone. She could do it her way, but not alone. In our living and in our dying we need community. Lynda saw a connection between the beginning and the ending of life, saying, "I began life with God and I will end it with God." I think both the beginning and the end are communal events. When we were born, parents, grandparents, neighbors, and strangers loved this baby and were ready to help. When we die, we likewise need a loving community to bless the ending of life in this world.

Worries about the End of Life

When we think about dying, a whole list of concerns comes into focus. Most of these worries relate to the way people will treat us. Mildred's dream is an example of that. "Will people pay attention to my needs? Will I be alone in an elevator with no one to care for me?" Lynda's worry about the end of life was a continuation of her lifelong concern: "Can I get everything done in time?"

High on the list of concerns is that we want to die with dignity. It was hospice training that helped me focus on dignity. It is an important gift that isn't unique to each individual. We need to respect the dying. Hospice insists that the focus is not the family, not our convenience, not the professional routine, but the patient. It's the little things that matter—a haircut, a shave, a closed door or pulled drape, cleanliness that eliminates an unpleasant odor. There aren't many individual preferences that we can't respect in the face of death.

One assumption needs to be challenged: that dignity means being left alone to take care of ourselves. Dignity is not self-sufficiency. We need to teach people that dignity is not lost if someone needs help, even in the bathroom. We have to do everything for a newborn child, including changing diapers, yet we regard the infant with respect that is without end. Dignity is not independence; it is about being respected; being loved. When our needs are met day and night, that is a privilege at life's beginning and ending. If our help is given with respect, it will be received with gratitude.

Of course the big worry is the anguish of dying. Medication can ease the pain, and loving caregivers can make each day easier.

But dying is not easy. The biggest burden is grief. We understand that when a loved one dies, the family grieves the loss. But the one who dies grieves the loss of loved ones too. In our dying, we grieve the loss of husband, wife, partner, children, parents, close friends. The one who is dying grieves as surely as those who survive. In dying, we also experience grief over the loss of our lives, our bodies, our calling. Medicine, social workers, caregivers, and theologians help, but none of these can make dying easy.

From the Christian perspective, death itself can best be understood from the point of view found in the Gospel of John. Why did people in power crucify Jesus? In Matthew, Mark, and Luke, it was the cleansing of the temple that infuriated the religious leaders and prompted them to persuade the Roman authorities to consider crucifixion. John's Gospel is different from the other three in that the incident that triggered the cross was Jesus's raising Lazarus from the grave. Jesus shouted, "Lazarus, come out!" (John 11:43). John continues:

> [Some] went to the Pharisees and told them what [Jesus] had done. So the chief priests and the Pharisees called a meeting of the council, and said, "What are we to do? This man is performing many signs. If we let him go on like this everyone will believe in him, and the Romans will come and destroy both our holy place and our nation."
>
> John 11:46-48

Gail O'Day in *The New Interpreter's Bible* points to the irony of the miracle at the grave of Lazarus and the plan at the Sanhedrin. Those who would kill Jesus are powerless before the One who raised Lazarus from the dead.[4]

The account of the Lazarus event was not written to explain the historical events of the early church, but those events were influenced by the cross. In the presence of Jesus Christ, death is not the victor. The gospel is life for followers of Jesus. In the

early church, people knew they could be put to death for following Jesus; nonetheless, they followed. Because of their faith, the
church survived the persecution. Because of the Lazarus miracle,
there is a church and a faith today.

The story of the raising of Lazarus tells us that in our violent
time, we need not fear. Will I celebrate that good news when
death charges in on me? I don't know how I will respond in
such a moment, but I am sure that John understood not only
the power of Jesus's raising Lazarus from the grave but also the
power of the risen Christ himself. The Christian faith isn't alone
in announcing this fearless vision. The twenty-third Psalm makes
the same claim: "Even though I walk through the darkest valley,
I fear no evil; for you are with me" (Ps. 23:4). This conviction
that we need not fear death enables us to embrace life's most
dangerous truths. If we have learned that lesson, it will sustain
us in both our living and in our dying.

The Blessing of Grief

A beautiful example for us to follow is seen in the
way Jackie's mother, Lynda, reached out in her dying to family,
colleagues in the mission, and those who had once disagreed
with her, and in the way she reached out to her grandson. It is
not unusual to see a family disintegrate in the days following the
funeral. But families also have a way of coming together after a
loved one dies. At retreats I often ask, "When were you most aware
of God?" A common thread that ties us together is death.

When a parent, spouse, child, or close friend dies, that is
when we are most acutely aware of God. Indeed, an awareness
of our calling is often linked to our grief. As her mother was
dying, Jackie realized that her calling now led her to work for a
doctorate so that she could help immigrant children adjust to a
new culture. Isaiah described how he was called by God to be a
prophet:

> In the year that King Uzziah died, I saw the Lord sitting on a
> throne, high and lofty. . . . Then I heard the voice of the Lord
> saying, "Whom shall I send, and who will go for us?" And I
> said, "Here am I; send me!"
>
> Isaiah 6:1, 8

In the shadow of the death of a beloved king, Isaiah was
called.

Throughout our lives, we are called to be an example to
others. The most important time for that witness is at the end
of our lives. If we can approach death with some measure of
faithfulness, all of those gathered around will be blessed. If, in
our dying, we show a shred of courage, truthfulness, and grace,
we will have been true to our calling. It's not an accident that
the largest portion of all the gospels is the passion narrative describing Jesus's death. In understanding why and how he died,
we understand the meaning of his life. The way we live and die
can also reveal life's meaning.

When death draws near, everyone is paying attention. Eleven
years after Lynda died, John wrote down every detail of his
grandmother's death and read his account in worship.

> Jackie beckoned, "The nurse says she's a lot worse." We all moved
> to the bedroom. We circled the . . . bed, holding hands. We
> stood silently watching her. I felt I could actually see a physical
> struggle between the will of her spirit and her body's impotent
> shell. She had things left to do—but not the capability. She
> wanted control—but not to usurp God's control. She wanted
> a legacy—but had to trust that she'd achieved it. She wanted
> order and discipline—but even the ordered life came to an end.
> I saw all of these struggles in every tiny, tortured twitch of her
> shapeless face.
>
> In a few minutes, her breathing became more difficult.
> Professionally, the nurse could do nothing; she held Jack's hand.

We all watched. The gasping ceased. After a brief lull, Paul spoke up. He seemed to be addressing the nurse, though the comments were clearly aimed at everyone. "Mother was always telling us what to do," he said. "Last night, she told us that at this moment we should all sing 'Amen.'" . . . Even I knew the words, and the tune, and their power. We sang with tears in our eyes. Then we sang another round for good measure.[5]

As she lay dying, unable to do or say anything, who she was became clear to John; he understood her lists, her legacy, her discipline, and her surrender to God. In her dying she touched us all, and as a result, we understand more clearly who we are called to be.

For Reflection

- If you ever saw someone die, describe what happened and how it affected you.
- When have you been most aware of God?
- How did a loved one's death have an impact on your life?

Lessons
from
Troas

Since we began this book with St. Paul, it seems appropriate to end with him. We can summarize this book by taking his experience in Troas as an example:

> They went through the region of Phrygia and Galatia, having been forbidden by the Holy Spirit to speak the word in Asia. When they had come opposite Mysia, they attempted to go into Bithynia, but the Spirit of Jesus did not allow them; so, passing by Mysia, they went down to Troas. During the night Paul had a vision: there stood a man of Macedonia pleading with him and saying, "Come over to Macedonia and help us." When he had seen the vision, we immediately tried to cross over to Macedonia, being convinced that God had called us to proclaim the good news to them.
>
> Acts 16:6-10

The ruins of the ancient city of Troas still stand on the western shore of what was Asia Minor in Paul's day. It was a frustrating journey that brought Paul and his followers to Troas. The Spirit didn't allow them to continue their mission in Asia, and when they tried to go to Bithynia, the Spirit didn't allow that either. I don't think Paul's vision occurred the night he arrived in Troas. Some scholars suggest he might have waited there for a year or more. Troas was a place for him to wait for the Spirit to lead. The Spirit did lead. Paul had a vision of a man pleading with him, "Come over to Macedonia and help us." We can learn four lessons from this text—lessons that we have discussed in this book.

First, we learn about our calling. On the Damascus Road, Paul was called to be an apostle. In time, that calling led him to establish churches through which, he believed, the gospel could be conveyed. After the Jerusalem Council, he became the bridge between Jewish and Greek Christians. In this text we see the next chapter of his calling, the mission to be in Macedonia instead of Asia. Roger, Jackie, Bink, and I have shared our calls and their development from one purpose to a string of larger goals. We see in Troas Paul's new mission frontier and learn to be aware of the next expression of our own calling.

Second, we learn how to wait with patience. You would think that Paul, having been rejected again and again, would have given up and returned to his home church in Antioch. That was simply not an option for him. He was called to establish the church in cities across Asia, and he was called to minister to Jew and Gentile. He had been led that far, and then he had to wait for the leading of the Spirit. In that waiting posture he had to accept the stop signs of the Spirit; the waiting meant that he would not at that time invent a mission priority, and that he had to have faith that the Spirit would provide a vision. We also are called to wait faithfully that the Spirit might continue to lead us.

Third, we learn about the community. The author of the book of Acts says, "When [Paul] had seen the vision, we immediately tried to cross over to Macedonia, being convinced that God had called us to proclaim the good news to them." That is an amazing sentence. One person was inspired by the Spirit, and the whole community acted on the vision immediately and together. Indeed the text says, "God called *us* to proclaim the good news to them" (italics added). The Spirit spoke to Paul, and the whole community was called as a result. Again, that community spirit is what we have been exploring in this book.

Fourth, it becomes apparent that this call to "come over and help us" was not just about Paul. Indeed, it wasn't even just about the community gathered in Troas. The ancient Macedonia was to become Europe. The Christian community spread across Europe—from prince to pope, from monks working the fields to serfs. Since Macedonia is our text, Europe is our focus. The Christian church took the place of the Roman Empire in Europe, just as Herod of the Christmas story had feared. This global church can be traced back to Paul, who woke in the middle of the night and then awakened the whole community to the new mission.

Having been called, let us move on, mile after mile, year after year. Let us faithfully wait for God's leading when we have lost our way. Let us rejoice when one of us catches a vision that shows us where God might be calling us. Let us try to cross over to a future that is totally foreign to us, confident that, out of our tiny mission, the Spirit will transform the world. All of that is possible because we are called for life.

Introduction

1. Douglas Schuurman, *Vocation: Discerning Our Callings in Life* (Grand Rapids: Eerdmans, 2004), xi.
2. Harold G. Koenig, *Purpose and Power in Retirement: New Opportunities for Meaning and Significance* (Philadelphia: Templeton Foundation Press, 2002), 13, 15.
3. Ibid., 18-19.
4. Ibid., 23.
5. Ibid., 78.
6. Robert G. Kemper, *Planning for Ministerial Retirement* (Cleveland: Pilgrim Press, 1988), 26-30.

Chapter 1, Who Is Called, by Whom, for What?

1. Walter Brueggemann, "Genesis," *Interpretation* (Atlanta: John Knox, 1982), 84.

Chapter 3, Community

1. "Mentor," *The World Book Encyclopedia*, vol. 13 (Chicago: Field Enterprises Educational Corporation, 1970), 335.

Chapter 4, Ebb Tide: The Transition to Retirement

1. Paul C. Clayton, *Letters to Lee: Mentoring the New Minister* (Herndon, VA: Alban Institute, 1999), 17-18.

2. David McClelland, "Human Motivation Theory," www. learnmanagement2.com/DavidMcClelland.htm (accessed November 14, 2007).
3. Annual Meeting of West Parish of Barnstable, West Barnstable, Mass., June 26, 2005.
4. Kemper, *Planning for Ministerial Retirement*, 35.
5. Clayton, *Letters to Lee*, 11.
6. Kemper, *Planning for Ministerial Retirement*, 35.
7. Harvey Cox, *On Not Leaving It to the Snake* (New York: Macmillan, 1967), ix, xiii.
8. *Ibid.*, xiv.

Chapter 5, Don't Just Stand There, Do Something

1. Emily Brandon, "Working Can Boost Your Health," *US News and World Report*, student edition (June 12, 2006), 48, 50.
2. Anne Tergesen, "Live Long and Prosper. Seriously," *Business Week*, student edition (June 27, 2006), 84.
3. Gene Cohen, Lecture at a meeting of the Living Arts Institute, Dennis, Mass., Oct. 20, 2007.
4. www.baroquemusic.org/bqxvivaldi.html.
5. Kemper, *Planning for Ministerial Retirement*, 38.

Chapter 6, It's Not All About Me

1. Velma Wallis. *Two Old Women: An Alaska Legend of Betrayal, Courage, and Survival* (New York: Harper Collins, 1993), xi.
2. *Ibid.*, 96.
3. *Ibid.*, 118.
4. *Ibid.*, 130.

Chapter 7, Don't Just Do Something, Stand There

1. Elisabeth Kübler-Ross and David Kessler, *Life Lessons: Two Experts on Death and Dying Teach Us about the Mysteries of Life and Living* (New York: Touchstone, 2002), 159.
2. Bill Clinton, *My Life* (New York: Knopf, 2004), 104.
3. Doris Kearns Goodwin, *Team of Rivals* (New York: Simon & Schuster, 2005).
4. David McCullough, *John Adams* (New York: Simon & Schuster, 2001).

Chapter 8, The Final Call

1. May Sarton, *A Reckoning: A Novel* (New York: W. W. Norton, 1978), 7-8.
2. Kübler-Ross and Kessler, *Life Lessons,* 141.
3. John S. Clayton, "The Old Missionary," sermon delivered at the Red Lodge Community Church (United Church of Christ), Red Lodge, Mont., Sept. 26, 1999, 6.
4. Gail R. O'Day, "John," *The New Interpreter's Bible,* vol. IX (Nashville: Abingdon, 1995), 699.
5. John S. Clayton, "The Old Missionary," 8-9.

BIBLIOGRAPHY

"Antonio Vivaldi." Baroque Composers and Musicians. www.baroquemusic.org/bqxvivaldi.html (accessed December 20, 2007).

Brandon, Emily. "Working Can Boost Your Health." *US News and World Report,* student edition, 12 June 2006, 48, 50.

Brueggemann, Walter. "Genesis." *Interpretation: A Bible Commentary for Teaching and Preaching.* Atlanta: John Knox, 1982.

Clayton, John S. "The Old Missionary" Sermon delivered at the Red Lodge Community Church (United Church of Christ), Red Lodge, Mont., September 26, 1999.

Clayton, Paul C. *Letters to Lee: Mentoring the New Minister.* Herndon, VA: Alban Institute, 1999.

Clinton, Bill. *My Life.* New York: Knopf, 2004.

Cohen, Gene. Lecture at a meeting of the Living Arts Institute, Dennis, Mass., Oct. 20, 2007.

Cox, Harvey. *On Not Leaving It To The Snake.* New York: Macmillan, 1967.

Goodwin, Doris Kearns. *Team of Rivals.* New York: Simon & Schuster, 2005.

Kemper, Robert G. *Planning for Ministerial Retirement.* New York: Pilgrim Press, 1988.

Koenig, Harold G. *Purpose and Power in Retirement: New Opportunities for Meaning and Significance.* Philadelphia: Templeton Foundation Press, 2003.

Kübler-Ross, Elisabeth, and David Kessler. *Life Lessons: Two Experts on Death and Dying Teach Us about the Mysteries of Life and Living.* New York: Touchstone, 2002.

"Mentor." *The World Book Encyclopedia,* vol. 13. Chicago: Field Enterprises Educational Corporation, 1970, 335.

McClelland, David. "Human Motivation Theory." www. learnmanagement2.com/DavidMcClelland.htm (accessed November 14, 2007).

McCullough, David. *John Adams.* New York: Simon & Schuster, 2001.

O'Day, Gail R. "John." *The New Interpreter's Bible,* vol. IX. Nashville: Abingdon, 1995.

Sarton, May. *A Reckoning: A Novel.* New York: W. W. Norton, 1978.

Schuurman, Douglas. *Vocation: Discerning Our Callings in Life.* Grand Rapids: Eerdmans, 2004.

Tergesen, Anne. "Live Long and Prosper Seriously." *Business Week,* student edition, 27 June 2006, 84.

Wallis, Velma. *Two Old Women: An Alaska Legend of Betrayal, Courage, and Survival.* New York: HarperCollins, 1993.

253.2084
C6227   LINCOLN CHRISTIAN COLLEGE AND SEMINARY

119502

3 4711 00182 5548